INSURRECTION

TO BELIEVE IS HUMAN
TO DOUBT, DIVINE

INSURREC✝ION

PETER ROLLINS

HOWARD BOOKS
A DIVISION OF SIMON & SCHUSTER, INC.

New York • London • Toronto • Sydney • New Delhi

Howard Books
A Division of Simon & Schuster, Inc.
1230 Avenue of the Americas
New York, NY 10020

First Howard Books hardcover edition October 2011

HOWARD and colophon are trademarks of Simon & Schuster, Inc.

For information about special discounts for bulk purchases,
please contact Simon & Schuster Special Sales at
1-866-506-1949 or business@simonandschuster.com.

The Simon & Schuster Speakers Bureau can bring authors
to your live event. For more information or to book an event,
contact the Simon & Schuster Speakers Bureau at
1-866-248-3049 or visit our website at www.simonspeakers.com.

Designed by Renato Stanisic

Manufactured in the United States of America

10   9   8   7   6   5   4   3   2   1

Library of Congress Cataloging-in-Publication Data
Rollins, Peter.
    Insurrection / Peter Rollins.
        p.   cm.
    Includes bibliographical references.
    1. Christian life. 2. Jesus Christ—Crucifixion. 3. Jesus Christ—Resurrection.
4. Emerging church movement. I. Title.
    BV4509.5.R66 2011
    248.4—dc23   2011016813

ISBN 978-1-4516-0900-4
ISBN 978-1-4516-0901-1 (ebook)

For Brian and Jill

PRO TANTO QUID RETRIBUAMUS

Contents

Contents

The Pauline question whether circumcision is a condition of justification seems to me in present-day terms to be whether religion is a condition of salvation.

—DIETRICH BONHOEFFER[1]

Introduction

There Is a Fire inside the Building; Please Step Inside

Each epoch in the life of the Church arises from the white-hot fires of a fundamental question, a question that burns away the husk that was once thought to be essential in order to reveal once more the revolutionary event heralded by Christ's Crucifixion and Resurrection. Such questions do not address the vast sea of disagreements that exist within the shared theological horizon of an era but challenge the very horizon itself. They place into question the various assumptions that these groups all take for granted. They cut across what is assumed, short-circuit what is hallowed, and, in so doing, appear on the scene as a profound threat to the very essence of Christianity. They offer us a unique opportunity to rethink what it means to be the Church, not merely critiquing the presently existing Church for failing to live up to its ideals, but rather for espousing the wrong ideals.

The first question of this kind was related to the issue of circumcision. At the very founding of the Church, a heated debate broke out concerning whether or not this outward sign was a requirement for Gentile converts. This was a controversial issue at the time, but when the dust finally settled, a decision had been made. New converts would not need to undergo circumcision in order to participate in the full life of the Church. This decision, known as the "Apostolic Decree," was revolutionary and helped to establish the unique identity of the Christian community. More than this, it helped bring to light the idea that faith concerned a total life transformation rather than some outward mark.

There have been various pivotal debates like this one over the life of the Church, debates that gave rise to monasticism, that provoked the split between Eastern and Western branches of Christianity, and that spawned the Protestant Reformation. Like the discussions concerning circumcision, each of these historical debates marked a radical transformation in the Church of its day. As such we may link them directly to what gave rise to the Apostolic Decree by calling them "Circumcision Questions."

Giving them this name not only links them directly to the first fundamental question that arose in the Christian community but also refers to the nature of these questions as such, for they are never concerned with addition (working out what needs to be added to the message as it currently stands) but with subtraction (debating what needs to be cut away). A circumcision question asks us to remove something previously thought of as vital in order to help unveil, in an apocalyptic way, the central scandal of Christianity.

In this book I suggest that we stand once more at the threshold of such a question, a question that houses the power to provoke a rupturing and re-configuring of the present manifestation of Christianity. It is an incendiary question that houses the very power to set the Church alight, burning away the rot to reveal that which cannot be consumed. This is why the task of working through a circumcision question can never be described as some project in constructive theology; it is a work of pyro-theology.

While circumcision questions attempt to bring us back to a central truth-event of faith, we must not confuse them with the reactionary movements that seek to return to the early Church—the Church in some more ancient, and supposedly purified, form. There are those who want to go back to the way the Church was before Constantine, when it is thought that religious authorities became extensions of the State. There is an attempt to return to the Church before the influence of Neo-Platonism when, those people say, Greek philosophy perverted the message. And there are even those who want to return to the Church before Paul—who some believe reduced the message of Christ to a set of rules and dogmas. Such moves, however, fall short, not because they go back too far, but because they fail to go back *far enough*.

The truly revolutionary move is not to chart a return to the early Church, but *to the event that gave birth to the early Church.*

The return called for by circumcision questions is not concerned with some stretching back into the past, for the event that gave birth to the early Church is present *now*. It is not lost in some long-forgotten era to be unearthed anew but rather dwells as an ever-present potential that we are invited to make actual in our bodies. In the aftermath of a circumcision question, an expression of Church life arises that may look utterly different from anything that went before it, yet it is fed by the same blood that pulsed through the old, remaining true to it by advancing boldly into the new.

So what is the question that presents itself at this time in the history of Christianity? What is this point from which we may gain the leverage to overturn the Church as it presently stands (in its conservative, liberal, evangelical, fundamentalist, and orthodox forms)?

The theologian Dietrich Bonhoeffer succinctly articulated the answer shortly before his execution by the Nazis. In a compilation of his personal correspondence entitled *Letters and Papers from Prison*, he wrote of how the question for us today is whether or not *religion* is necessary in order to participate fully in the life testified to by Christ.[2]

For Bonhoeffer, religion at its most basic defined a particular way of thinking about and relating to God, a way of approaching God as the solution to problems such as fear, ignorance, or despair. He wrote of the next epoch in Church life as one that would utterly transcend this impotent God whose only job is to provide us with a psychological crutch (what we will call the God of religion, or the religious God) and usher in what he called "religionless Christianity."[3] Bonhoeffer was executed before he was able to develop his project, and we are left with only fragments of his vision, fragments that are pregnant with possibility.

In *Insurrection*, I endeavor to outline what this radical expression of a faith beyond religion might look like and how it has the power to give birth to a radically new form of Church, one with the power to renew, reform or even transcend the present constellation of conservative, liberal, evangelical, fundamentalist, and orthodox communities.

This work of pyro-theology will involve outlining the present understanding of God, exploring the way Crucifixion and Resurrection open up a different reality, and charting what might arise should we be courageous enough to step into this reality.

The following will not be an easy read; many will find it disturbing, for some of the things we hold precious will be attacked from the very outset. But it is written with a firm conviction that we must not be afraid to burn our sacred temples in order to discover what, if anything, remains.

Indeed, perhaps it is not what remains after the fire has died that is true, but rather the fire itself. If so, then we need to take the words of Spanish anarchist Buenaventura Durruti seriously when he boldly declares: *The only church that illuminates is a burning one.*[4]

Part 1

CRUCIFIXION

═══

Eloi, Eloi, lama sabachthani.

—THE WORDS OF JESUS ACCORDING TO THE GOSPELS
OF MATTHEW AND MARK

Only an atheist can be a good Christian;
only a Christian can be a good atheist.

—ERNEST BLOCH

===

I'm a Christian! I'm a Christian!

Every Sunday the pastor would stand at the front of his Church and with a booming voice finish his rousing sermon with a plea:

"Each week I go to a nearby town and serve the poor, the oppressed, and the downtrodden; what do you do? How do you show your compassion to those in need?"

People would applaud the minister's closing remarks and everyone would wave him off at the end of the service as he hurried away in his little car.

The truth, however, was that each week he would go to a golf course and play a leisurely eighteen holes away from his congregation, family, and friends.

This deception had been going on for years, but eventually it came to the attention of some angels. They were furious at his lies and reported the situation directly to God.

After a little consideration, God said to the angels, "I will visit with this minister on Sunday and teach him a lesson he'll never forget."

Sure enough, next Sunday, God showed up at the Church. Yet again, the minister informed his congregation that he was going to go serve the poor before leaving for the golf course.

This time however, God intervened. When the minister took his first shot, the ball took off, flew through the air, bounced onto the green, and dropped into the hole.

The minister was amazed. At the second hole the same thing happened. And the third. And the fourth. Right through to the last hole.

With his last stroke, the minister sliced the ball badly, but still it curved around and, like all the others, found the hole in one.

All the while the angels in heaven watched what took place in utter disbelief. By the time God returned they shouted, "I thought you were going to punish the minister for all his lies, but instead you gave him the perfect round of golf!"

"That may be true," replied God with a smile, "but ask yourself this: Who is he going to tell?"

I Desire Your Desire

Believing that there is some Supreme Being above and beyond the world we experience, a Being who loves us and cares about what happens in our lives, is natural. We want to believe. To understand this let us reflect upon the nature of desire.

Most of us will agree that the things we love are not as important to us as the people we love. We desire a myriad of things in life (such as wealth, health, and longevity), but in the midst of these, we will be quick to point out that our loved ones stand over and above them all. Those few individuals who bring life and light to the very depths of our being elicit the most profound and intense longings in our heart.

And yet, true as this description may be, it is also incomplete and inadequate. For when we speak of those we love as more desirable than everything else that might capture our attention, we end up subtly placing them on the same level as everything else we desire.

If we simply long for our partner in a more intense and inflamed way than a promotion at work, a holiday in the Bahamas, or a home by the beach, we end up treating them in much the same way—as one more thing we want. Such a description of those we love, while disguising itself as a compliment, does them a profound injustice, failing to delve into their unique and transcendent place in our life. For our desire for those we love is not merely superior to all other desires, it is of a fundamentally different kind.

Imagine that most painful of experiences, the loss of our beloved: Most of us know what it is like to be scorched by that black sun, to lose someone for whom we would gladly lose everything to save. If we take a moment to reflect upon such a loss in our own life, we find that when we lose the one we love more than life itself, we do not simply lose something we desire; we begin to lose *the very ability to desire.*

In other words, when we lose our beloved, we find that the other things that once tempted us lose their seductive power. Thoughts of promotions, vacations, and new homes lose all of their glittering appeal. A chilling melancholy slowly envelops us, fading our once vibrant world into various shades of gray.

In these times, we discover that our beloved is not simply the object of our desire, but the very source of it. In that dark dungeon of despair, we find that the other is the one who invests our activities with meaning and significance. Any of our achievements, while once meaningful to us, now signify nothing.

What we learn from this traumatic experience is that the loss of our beloved results in our world being cut adrift from its sun and descending into ever-greater darkness. For more than being the mere objects of our deepest desire, those we love are the ones who birth and sustain our very ability to desire.

It is not then our beloved's mere existence that lights up our life with meaning; it is our beloved's desire for us that has this luminous effect. We might even still be with the one we love, but if we feel that they no longer love us, we experience the profound pain and suffering described above. In contrast, the one we love may be far away, and yet their longing and desire for us can sustain us in their absence. So then, what we really desire, what I really desire, is the desire of those I desire.

Ever Get the Feeling That No One Is Watching You?

The idea that what we desire is the other's desire is succinctly captured in the story that opens this chapter. Here we are confronted with the initially counterintuitive idea that something we would assume to be a reason for personal delight (the perfect golf game) could actually lead us into a state of profound despair (by being witnessed by no one).

The pastor's punishment lay not in what actually took place but in the fact that he was unable to share it. He was punished not with a direct misfortune but with the indirect misfortune of being unable to share something fortunate. This story presents to us the psychological reality that our pleasure is intimately interwoven with the pleasure (or pain) of those around us. Understanding this can help us unlock something fundamental about the nature of human desire—namely, that the most sought after material in the universe is not some precious metal or limited resource but rather the attention of those whom we desire. We long to be seen by the other and acknowledged by them in some way. Yet this most precious of materials proves to be frustratingly ethereal, elusive, and fleeting.

When we take a moment to understand this, we can begin to perceive how even our most intimate and private fantasies are never really for us alone but are indirectly addressed to another. In the theater of our mind, we may stage a scene in which we are a great musician, a world-famous celebrity, a powerful secret agent, or a beautiful model, but we must remember that there is also an audience watching what we have produced and directed—those for whom we are staging this fantasy.

If we ask ourselves who this spectator is, we may find that it is someone who bullied us in school, a parent who didn't think we would amount to anything, or some individual we are attracted to and yet who seems utterly oblivious to our existence. This is something we see in the film *The Social Network* where Mark Zuckerberg's (Jesse Eisenberg) motivation for setting up Facebook is directly connected to a failed relationship with Erica Albright (Rooney Mara). This spectator is often little more than an image we have in our mind (for instance, this person could be long dead in reality), but he or she is the one who invests our fantasies and achievements with their excessive pleasure (i.e., the pleasure we get that is beyond the mere satisfaction of basic needs). Whether it is that person's love, affection, regret, or jealousy we seek, these are all evidence of us evoking and colonizing the other's desire.

Early in our lives, we learn that we can never fully capture other people's desire, at least not for any sustained and prolonged period of time. As infants we quickly discover that our parents have interests that lie far beyond us. In a typical family environment, we are faced with the reality that we are not the center of our parents' universe. They have jobs, friends, and other interests that draw their gaze away from us and steal their attention. It may be painful, but accepting this is a vital part of growing up. Indeed a myriad of problems are known to arise if the desire of our parents is too intense and focused upon us. We must be weaned off our obsessive desire for our parents' desire in order to mature and find other relationships outside the closed circuit of the family.

This process of desiring our parents' desire is mirrored as we begin to develop serious relationships beyond those of our immediate family. Our partner comes to partially replace our parents as the one whose desire we desire, and yet we again discover early on that we can never be the only one that our beloved's gaze alights upon. In the initial stages of a relationship, the two individuals may feel that all their wants and needs are met in the other. But as time goes by, the exigencies of daily life impact the relationship, and both find other activities they want to pursue. In a healthy partnership, this transformation can help to bring about a more well-rounded and mature union, but it can also be a painful process, one that we often try desperately to avoid.

In light of all this, it is perfectly understandable that we would find ourselves desiring someone who would love us unconditionally and absolutely. An individual who would never cease caring for us, who would never leave our side, never die, and never tire of our presence. If it is true that we find meaning through the loving gaze of another and that the loss of this love leads to great suffering, then it is only natural that we would desire the gaze of one who would forever cradle us and never forsake us.

Regardless of *whether or not such a being actually exists*, the desire is then a perfectly natural one. We find great solace in the idea of someone presiding over the world who guarantees that our small and seemingly insignificant lives are being seen and cherished. To believe is human.

It is in light of this that we can appreciate the power of Voltaire's famous statement, "If God did not exist, it would be necessary to invent him." In short, God is rendered into a psychological crutch, a being we affirm in order to sleep better at night.

Making Myself Believe

This does not mean that people's belief in God always arises from a psychological need. But while, in theory, we can make the distinction between a belief in God that does not function as a crutch and one that does, it is much more difficult to work out the distinction in the reality of people's lives. Part of the difficulty relates to the way that belief itself is formed and transmitted. Something that is expressed in the following anecdote from Northern Ireland that was told during the Troubles:

> At the height of the conflict in Northern Ireland, a major piece of funding was secured from the European Union in order to help train the police force (the RUC). As a result, some of the RUC's top officers were sent over to America to work alongside the FBI and the CIA in a series of team-building exercises.
>
> When they arrived, the officers met with their counterparts and were then driven to a large forest for some team-building exercises. Each group was given instructions to go into the forest and retrieve a rabbit.
>
> The FBI went first. Ten men, fully armed, threw canisters of tear gas into the forest before storming through the trees. After about ten minutes of intense shouting, the sound of a single gunshot rang through the air. Moments later the FBI returned with a small rabbit, a bullet hole through the center of its head.
>
> Next the CIA had their opportunity to prove themselves. In contrast to the FBI, they disappeared into the forest without a sound.

Thirty minutes passed without any sound. Eventually the faint echo of a single twig snapping broke the silence. Shortly afterwards the CIA emerged from the undergrowth with a lifeless rabbit, not a mark on its body.

Finally it was the RUC's turn. The men put on their flak jackets, loaded their weapons, and charged into the forest with batons raised. Eventually they emerged from amidst the trees dragging behind them a huge bear. The instructor shook his head in disbelief and said, "Firstly, you were in there for three weeks; and secondly, that's not a rabbit, that's a bear."

But the largest RUC man simply smiled at the instructor, then turned to the bear and looked deep into its eyes. Immediately the bear began to tremble, looked at the instructor, and shouted, "I'm a rabbit! I'm a rabbit!"

It is, of course, clear that the bear's claim is not the outcome of some intellectual conviction but rather arises as the result of external force, a strategy that is mirrored throughout history in the acts of various powerful political and religious groups. History is sadly littered with examples where the Church has used physical pressure to evoke belief. At its most horrifying there have even been times when religious authorities sanctioned the use of torture and execution in order to bring about confessions of belief. For example, during the Inquisition, which began around the late fifteenth century, whole communities were forced to change their religious allegiance or face severe persecution.

Unfortunately such examples of outward cruelty are simply the most extreme and perverse expression of techniques that we still witness in more clandestine forms today. It is not unusual to find people who have undergone intense forms of psychological coercion in church—those who have been bombarded with fiery sermons detailing vivid images of eternal punishment for those who would refuse to accept Christ. In more contemporary evangelical churches, this approach has largely been replaced by a type of apologetics designed to convince listeners that, without God, there is no meaning to life, no moral code to live by, and no reason to value one's existence. This is no argument that hell awaits those who do not believe, but rather that those who do not believe already dwell in a type of hell.

This technique can prove particularly effective when deep suffering and desperation strike a person; it is not uncommon for someone to be coaxed into a confession of faith on his or her deathbed or upon his or her return from the deathbed of one they love.

There is, however, an important difference between the religious confession that is wrought through persecution and the religious confession that is evoked through images of a world without meaning. For while the former, like that of the bear in the above story, is addressed to other people, the later is addressed to the self. That is, the person who affirms God through fear of persecution makes the claim in order to convince another, while people who affirm God through fear of hell or meaninglessness seek to convince themselves.

It might seem strange that someone can be convinced of an idea as a result of external force, but this is actually one of the primary ways that we come to hold any belief. There is a famous experiment in which someone was hypnotized and then told to carry an open umbrella around the room. When they were taken out of hypnosis, they were asked to explain why they had performed the act, and in response, the individual offered up a number of explanations, all of which betrayed the fact that they thought the desire was an internal one, not caused by external factors. This process, which has since been proven time and time again, is called *rationalization*. Rationalization involves an individual making up reasons for a behavior or belief that covers over the real (often external) cause.

We see this process most clearly in children, for they are less able to hide the process of rationalization than adults. Children will think up a lot of false reasons to justify their actions when they have been caught doing something that they were not supposed to do—reasons not only designed to justify their actions to their parents, but also to themselves.

We also see this play out in the way that we tend to read books and watch programs that agree with our already existing worldview. We often use the information we have just learned to pretend to others and ourselves that we have chosen our beliefs because of that information, instead of admitting that we believed beforehand and simply used the information to back it up.

We should not get too caught up here in trying to work out the extent to which one believes because of evidence, socialization, or psychological need. At this point we should simply take a little time to reflect upon how the idea of a Supreme Reality (which will manifest itself in a multitude of different ways—including post-theistic forms, such as claims to Destiny, Fate, or a Cosmic Principle) provides great psychological comfort, and therefore is easy to spread and difficult to question.

God as a Function

Near the end of his life, the theologian and activist Dietrich Bonhoeffer became concerned that the Christian understanding of God had been largely reduced to the status of a psychological crutch. He described this understanding of God as deus ex machina.

This phrase, which literally means "God out of the machine," originally refers to a technique used in ancient Greece in which a person would be lowered onto the stage via a mechanism in order to signify the introduction of a supernatural being. The process, however, got a bad name whenever many second-rate playwrights used this device in a rather lazy and arbitrary way. If they wanted to kill off a character, create a new challenge for the main antagonist to overcome, or resolve a conflict in the plot, they would simply wheel in a god to make it happen. In this way, the supernatural being was not an organic part of the story but rather an intrusive presence employed purely to move the plot along or resolve an issue.

As a result of this, the term *deus ex machina* came to mean the introduction of something that was not part of the internal logic of an unfolding story but instead a clumsy device dropped into the narrative purely to perform a specific role.

One of the most infamous examples of deus ex machina in television history is from the long-running soap opera *Dallas*. At the end of season six, Patrick Duffy, who played the character Bobby Ewing, wanted to leave the show. As a result, the writers, as one might expect, killed off the character. However, after the death, it became obvious that he was one of the most popular characters on the show, and the ratings quickly began to suffer. After convincing Patrick Duffy to return, they ended season seven with one of the most surreal cliffhangers in television history. Moments before the credits roll, we see Bobby Ewing's widow wake up and approach the bathroom. When she opens the door, she is shocked, as are the viewers, to find her husband alive and well, standing in the shower. The reason? Season seven was nothing but *his wife's dream*.

Here the dream sequence functions as a device that has nothing to do with the internal logic of the story. The dream sequence was "dropped" into the *Dallas* narrative simply to help resolve a problem in the story. Contrast this with Christopher Nolan's film *Inception*. Unlike the dream sequence in *Dallas*, which was not part of the structure of the overarching narrative, dreaming is central to the logic of *Inception*. While in *Dallas* it is a foreign notion imposed upon the soap opera's universe, in *Inception* the dreaming is an integral part of the universe.

For Bonhoeffer, the Church approached God as a deus ex machina. God was merely an idea clumsily dropped into our world in order to fulfill a task. God was introduced into the world on our terms in order to resolve a problem rather than expressing a lived reality. The result is a God who simply justifies our beliefs and helps us sleep comfortably at night. God is brought into the picture only when we face a problem of some kind that doesn't lend itself to solution by other means. In Bonhoeffer's view, this God plays the same meager role as the supernatural beings in third-rate Greek plays.

The God of Philosophy

When faced with the idea that everything is fleeting, that our lives are insignificant, that everyone we know will turn to dust, that no one will remember us, and that everything we have accomplished will be forgotten in the unending march of time, we can despair. The thought that our cosmic golf game, no matter how beautifully played, is being observed by no one can prove too much for us to bear.

In order to protect ourselves from this experience, we are tempted to relate to God as the cosmic spectator who gives life meaning.

Consider how many of us turn to the religious life in times of trouble. Here the deus ex machina is something that comforts us in moments of crisis or when we are faced with a phenomenon we cannot describe. This is perfectly natural. We desire a being that can be wheeled in to either protect us in a way that our family, friends, and community can't, or to give a supernatural explanation for what we cannot understand. This God is, however, a concept that we create—what Pascal called "the God of philosophy." Such is the temptation to embrace this God of human thought that the apostle Paul wrote,

> *See to it that no one takes you captive through hollow and deceptive philosophy, which depends on human tradition and the basic principles of this world rather than on Christ.*[1]

This God of philosophy is ultimately impotent. When it takes center stage, faith is reduced to an idea that helps us cope with life, and theology is reduced to a form of theodicy (the discipline that seeks to provide reasons why God allows suffering and evil). As a result we are left with nothing but a hollow and deceptive philosophy. Here the God of philosophy—the deus ex machina—rises to the ascendancy, and we lose sight of the world-transforming message of Christianity.

Because of our natural fears concerning life and its impending end, convincing people to embrace God as a crutch can be so very easy. It is no surprise that those preachers with perfect smiles and white suits fill stadiums week after week with their slick sales talk concerning a being that ensures everything will work out well in the end. It's easy to convince us to believe because we want certainty. We have a deep-seated longing to confirm our desire for an ordered universe: a universe that makes sense, a universe in which we are special, valued, and eternal. And on top of it all, like the child who rationalizes her behavior, we have a deep desire to convince ourselves that we believe for reasons other than mere psychological need. Hence we will often seek out evidence to support the already existing belief and then pretend that our belief arose from the evidence.

But the result is a faith that exists only at the very margins of our life, a faith that only has something to offer when we feel depressed, or scared, or when we face death. But what if someone actually enjoys life and embraces it? God as a psychological crutch would seem to have nothing to offer at all. The only option left for the apologist who is confronted by someone who actually enjoys life is to attempt to show that they are really in denial and crying out for this God in a disavowed way. If they cannot succeed in convincing the happy person that they are really unhappy, then they have nothing left to offer and must reject them as one caught up in rebellion, deception, and defiance.

While Bonhoeffer believed that the God of religion had run its course, the reality would appear somewhat different. Some of the biggest organizations in the world are religious, and there would seem to be no end to people filling the collection plates of those who claim to have the solution. There is an army of individuals who eagerly support their ministries, buy their books and fill their pews. Getting people to believe in some form of deus ex machina is as easy as getting children to believe in Santa Claus.

In contrast, inviting people to open up to the experience of doubt and unknowing is much more tricky: The religious God provides us with such stability that the experience of losing it involves nothing less than the horrifying experience of being forsaken. Such a journey into darkness can be so unnatural and frightening that we avoid this narrow path at all costs, even turning violently on anyone who would encourage us to do so.

The one who commits themselves to the task of helping people really enter into doubt, unknowing, and ambiguity needs to be ten, twenty, even a hundred times better than those who sell certainty. They have got to be prepared to walk a difficult and often dangerous path if they wish to invite people into this murky and uncertain world, for in doing so they bring to the surface a whole host of anxieties that we spend so much of our time and resources repressing. It is understandable that certain pastors fill stadiums with people longing to solidify their already established desires, reconverting people to what they have converted to so many times before. Getting people to believe is easy precisely because it is so natural for us. Any persuasive human can do it—and even make some money in the process. But to truly unplug from the God of religion, with all the anxieties and distress this involves, takes courage.

Indeed, one could say that it takes God.

CHAPTER TWO

To Believe Is Human; to Doubt, Divine

Long ago there was an old sage who was deeply respected by the people. But he was also feared, for he was known to have a short temper, wild penetrating eyes, and strange, almost supernatural powers.

While he generally kept away from the city, he would sometimes be seen walking through the markets in the middle of the day with a lit torch held high in one hand, a bowl overflowing with water in the other hand, and a huge sword strapped to his side.

The citizens knew to keep out of his way and never once asked why he carried these objects everywhere he went. But one day a small group of travelers saw the sage and, not knowing who he was, mocked him.

"Old man," said one, "why do you stumble around in the middle of the day with a torch, a bowl of water, and a sword strapped to your side?"

"Maybe he's blind," laughed his friend.

*"Or maybe he is afraid that thieves will steal his precious water,"
shouted another.*

*The sage stopped for a moment and listened to them as they
laughed, then in an instant he threw the torch into their midst and
said, "With these flames I consume heaven!"*

*Then he spilled the water onto the parched earth before them
and cried, "With this water I extinguish hell!"*

*Finally he unsheathed his sword and approached the travelers,
who were now silent.*

*"And with this sword," whispered the sage with sacred convic-
tion, "I lay waste to God."*[1]

When God Became an Atheist

Religious belief, in its affirmation of the deus ex machina, helps
to provide us with shelter from the bitter storms of life. By tap-
ping into our natural desire for meaning, understanding, order,
and purpose, it has a seductive and tempting call. Because of this,
such belief is very natural and very human.

It is in light of this that the Crucifixion of Christ can strike
within us such a discordant tone, for here we witness more than
the horror of an innocent man being tortured and killed. We see
more than an act of political injustice or religious violence. On the
cross we are confronted with God losing the security of God.

If this were exclusively a description of some innocent man being
executed, we would be at a loss to understand the world-wide historical

power that the event continues to hold for so many. Yet to go further than this and read it as a concrete manifestation of the idea that love will be violently opposed by hate also fails to go far enough. What we miss in such readings is the true scandal of the Cross. It is only when we see the Crucifixion as the moment where God loses everything that we begin to glimpse the true theological significance of the event.

What we witness here is a form of atheism: not intellectual—Christ directly addresses God as he dies—but a felt loss of God. In the Gospels according to Matthew and Mark we read of Christ crying out in agony, "My God, my God, why have you forsaken me?"[2] This is a profoundly personal, painful, and existential atheism. Not an atheism that arises from some rational reflection upon an absence of divinity but rather one that wells up from the trauma of personally experiencing that absence. It is not some precursor to the atheism of people like Richard Dawkins. It is not a comfortable theoretical rejection of the divine. Christ expresses a deeply felt loss, one that has more in common with the atheism we see expressed in Friedrich Nietzsche, whose blood-curdling proclamation of God's death in the nineteenth century was deeply felt. On the cross, Christ undergoes the deepest, most radical form of divine loss, one that is *experienced*.

It is this scandal that is so resisted and repressed in the contemporary Church. The existing Church seems dedicated today to reducing the Crucifixion to mere mythology. While this is something that takes place across the different traditions, it finds its most extreme expression in fundamentalism.

A mythology can be described as a narrative that brings meaning, order, and stability to our fragmented experience. At its most basic, it is a narrative that reassures us everything makes sense, everything has a purpose, and everything is in its place. When confronted by chaos and unknowing, a mythology is a story that enables us to cover over the cracks. Creation mythologies, for instance, offer us a way of grasping onto that most perplexing of mysteries (why is there something rather than nothing), reassuring us that the universe is grounded in some higher order.

It is perfectly natural for us to construct mythologies in order to make sense of our fragmented and complex world. However, it is a mistake to read the Crucifixion in this way. By committing to a mythological reading, the fundamentalists strip away the central scandal of the Cross, domesticating the truth we find there. By approaching the Crucifixion in this way, the church integrates it into a larger cosmic narrative and thus betrays it. The result is nothing more than a roller-coaster version of Christianity—one that offers a voyeuristic sense of danger robbed of its trauma. When the Crucifixion is understood as offering the security of meaning, rather than being the site where meaning is ripped away, then any experience of doubt, unknowing, and loss that is found there is eclipsed by an even greater certainty that everything is really fine.

The Crucifixion, however, stands in opposition to mythology. It is a reflection of the experience in which we lose any sense of being connected with a higher truth or reality. Something we see foreshadowed in the book of Ecclesiastes. Is not the Teacher's cry, "Meaningless, meaningless, everything is meaningless," a precursor to Christ's cry of dereliction on the cross? This event thus speaks of an explosion that fundamentally breaks apart mythology in all of its various forms (spiritual, social, and political).

The Crucifixion signals an experience in which all that grounds us and gives us meaning collapses. On the Cross, Christ is rejected by his friends, betrayed by the religious authorities, and crucified by the political leaders. We witness here, in the starkest of terms, the loss of all those structures that ground us and give us the comfort that life makes sense. More than this, Christ experiences the loss of that which grounds each of these realms—God.

To participate in the Crucifixion is to experience the breaking apart of the various mythologies we use to construct and make sense of our world. The Crucifixion experience is nothing less than the taking place of the Real. It is the incoming of that which cannot be contained in our various mythologies, that which ruptures them and calls them into question.

Forsakenness as Faith

All religions have adherents who profoundly experience the loss of meaning, and all religions offer varying explanations for this. Some speak of it representing a test, others claim that it is a result of sin, and still others say that it comes from an inability to grasp the bigger picture because of our humanity. But here Christianity offers a fundamentally different response: This loss is not an experience one has in relation to one's faith, but rather is a central expression of one's faith. It is not something one feels toward Christianity; when one feels this loss, one stands fundamentally *within* Christianity.

All religions have generated their atheistic oppositions, but in the Crucifixion this atheistic opposition is brought into the very heart of the Christian faith. It is no longer to be thought of as a response one makes to faith but is part of that faith's very expression. As such this negation is not something that we must fight or merely endure; rather, it is something that we *must* step into and courageously embrace.

It is easy for us to take the experience of God's absence as a rejection of God's presence and either celebrate it or bemoan it, depending upon one's position. But a properly Christological reflection should lead us to see the felt experience of God's absence as *the fundamental way of entering into the presence of God.* For if being a Christian involves participating in the Crucifixion, then it means undergoing this earth-shattering loss. While various religious systems provide a place for this painful experience of unknowing (as a test, as something to endure, or something to overcome), in Christianity when one is crushed by a deep, existential loss of certainty, one finds oneself in Christ.

Domesticating Christ's Cry

In a desire to silence the true horror of Christ's cry of dereliction, many have claimed that he was really just quoting Psalm 22 and was therefore affirming the entire content of that psalm—a psalm which, in its totality, expresses deep belief. So, they claim, his cry of dereliction was really a shorthand description of belief, comfort, and security.

This perspective, however, fails to take into account the significance of the fact that the cry recorded in the Gospels of Matthew and Mark is put in Jesus' native tongue (Aramaic) rather than in the psalm's original Hebrew. In the Jewish faith, the Hebrew Scriptures are read, memorized, and recalled in the original language, not one's native tongue, so while this cry might be inspired by the psalm, the words reflect a person's heartfelt cry of agony and loss rather than some mere quote. To read it otherwise would be to view it as part of some kind of cosmic theatrical show, a phrase that provides the whole Crucifixion scene with a sense of drama and despair all the while offering a wink that tells us everything is really fine.

We must instead give this cry its full theological and existential weight. We must read it with all of its horror and potency. It is a cry that comes from one cut off from all grounding in a deeper reality, one who has lost all sense of meaning, all mythological frames. It is a cry that exposes us to a man utterly destitute.

Here, right at the heart of Christianity, God despairs of God.

From the Religious Sacrifice to the Sacrifice of Religion

The Crucifixion takes the experience of Jesus in the Garden of Gethsemane to a whole new level. In order to understand this, let us read about what took place the night Jesus was arrested:

*Then Jesus went with his disciples to a place called Gethse-
mane, and he said to them, "Sit here while I go over there and
pray." He took Peter and the two sons of Zebedee along with
him, and he began to be sorrowful and troubled. Then he said to
them, "My soul is overwhelmed with sorrow to the point of death.
Stay here and keep watch with me."*

*Going a little farther, he fell with his face to the ground and
prayed, "My Father, if it is possible, may this cup be taken from
me. Yet not as I will, but as you will."*

*Then he returned to his disciples and found them sleeping.
"Could you men not keep watch with me for one hour?" he asked
Peter. "Watch and pray so that you will not fall into temptation.
The spirit is willing, but the body is weak."*

*He went away a second time and prayed, "My Father, if it is
not possible for this cup to be taken away unless I drink it, may
your will be done."*

*When he came back, he again found them sleeping, because
their eyes were heavy. So he left them and went away once more
and prayed the third time, saying the same thing.*

*Then he returned to the disciples and said to them, "Are you
still sleeping and resting? Look, the hour is near, and the Son of
Man is betrayed into the hands of sinners. Rise, let us go! Here
comes my betrayer!"³*

In the Garden of Gethsemane, we witness the very essence of
the religious sacrifice—for here we witness how Jesus is ready and
willing to lose everything for God. While many people are content

to believe in order to feel better about themselves, few are willing to give up everything for this belief, demonstrating their gratefulness through absolute devotion and the offering up of everything they are, even up to, and including, martyrdom.

However, while this sacrifice for religion can initially seem to demonstrate the highest watermark of Christian giving, there is a move that transcends it; on the Cross, we find an even more radical loss. While in the Garden of Gethsemane we witness the sacrifice *for* religion, on the Cross, we come face to face with the sacrifice of religion.

In the sacrifice for religion, Christ loses everything for God, while in the sacrifice of religion Christ loses everything *including* God.

Let me be more specific: What is lost here is a way of relating to God as deus ex machina, as some being "out there" who ensures life makes sense. On the Cross, Christ becomes the absolute outsider. Everything that has supported him thus far has been stripped away. The religious system of the day sought his execution, the political system happily provided it, and his social circle quickly abandoned him. All that would ground him had been fundamentally shaken apart. There is no support here for Christ. On the Cross he is left naked, alone, dying.

God on the Gallows

This expression of Christ finds a modern literary expression in Elie Wiesel's post-Holocaust reflection *Night*. There Wiesel tells of a horrifying experience in which he is forced to watch the hanging of some prisoners in a Nazi concentration camp. Among the victims there is a young child. The child, unlike the men, is too light for a quick death, and instead his body writhes helplessly against the rope as his life is slowly and painfully extinguished. During this experience Wiesel hears someone in the camp shout out in despair, "Where is God, where is He?" During the execution everyone in the camp is forced to walk past the gallows where the child hangs. At the sight of this boy being robbed of life, Wiesel begins to weep. It is then that we read:

Behind me, I heard the same man asking: Where is God now? And I heard a voice within me answer him: . . . Here He is—He is hanging here on this gallows.[4]

This claim that God is hanging on the gallows is no standard denial of God. It is rather the rejection of a way of approaching God, it is the rejection of a religious view of God. The religious God has died on the gallows. The God who justifies our various mythologies, the God who tells us everything is going to work out well in the end.

Is this not how we should also read the Cross?

Where is God? Where is He now?

Here He is—He is hanging here on this Cross.

Participating in Christ's Death

In contrast to those who would see the experience of this loss as something to be endured and others who would claim that such feelings expose Christianity as false, we find the staggering message of the Cross: *Radical doubt, suffering, and the sense of divine forsakenness are central aspects of Christ's experience and thus a central part of what it means to participate in Christ's death.* The moment we feel the loss of all that once gave us meaning is not a time in which we are set free from Christ, nor is it a moment where we fall short of Christ: *It is the time when we stand side by side with Christ.*

To believe in the Crucifixion means nothing less than participating in it. We miss something crucial if we take the biblical witness as a mere signpost that points to a distant time in history. Christian belief in the Crucifixion is not about accepting some historical event; we are not invited to merely affirm or contemplate the death of Jesus on the cross, but to *undergo* that death in our own lives. And just as Christ was cut off from everything that grounded him, so our participation in Crucifixion will involve the same troubling, terrifying process.

Losing the God of Religion

To lose that which grounds us and provides us with meaning involves nothing less than losing the God of religion in whatever form it manifests itself in our life. This does not require ceasing to believe intellectually in some overarching principle that guides us, but rather it means losing the psychological power that such a principle possesses for us. Like Jesus, we too must make the journey from Gethsemane to Golgotha, a journey in which we pass from the sacrifice for religion (where we give up everything for God) to the sacrifice of religion itself (where we give up everything *including* God).

In the sacrifice of religion, we lose all the security that any deus ex machina might provide for us. In this dark hour, when the very earth beneath us gives way, we experience utter desolation.

While the sacrifice of religion itself involves an experience of desolation, we would be mistaken to think that the experience of desolation leads us into the sacrifice of religion. The experience of profound pain and suffering does not necessarily lead to the psychological collapse of the religious God. It is always possible to provide an explanation for our suffering that integrates into our already existing mythologies rather than breaking them open. Take the famous exchange between Elizabeth Anscombe and Ludwig Wittgenstein: It is said that Anscombe commented, "I can understand why people once believed that the sun revolved around the earth."

In response, Wittgenstein said, "Why is that?"

Anscombe looked up, pointed to the sky, and said, "Well, it looks like it does."

"Yes, yes," Wittgenstein replied. "But tell me, what would it look like if it was the other way around?"[5]

How we understand the suffering and pain of our lives will

depend upon the mythology we bring to it. This is why the experience of the Cross can be called a sacrifice rather than a mere loss, for there is something within us that must be courageous enough to let go. Often the more we suffer, the more we will want to hold onto our religious ideas, the more we will pull back from the brink of that sacred nihilism expressed in the Cross. We will want to repress the experience that everything that has sustained us thus far is inadequate, grasping anything that will either provide a reason for our suffering (apologetics) or help us avoid it altogether (distractions). When we suffer, there will always be an army of Job's comforters who attempt to save our mythologies, and like Job, we must resist them.

Who Is Number One?

Just as Christ is cut off from his own essence on the Cross, so our loss of the deus ex machina does not involve the letting go of some foreign power external to ourselves, but rather involves giving up that which is fully a part of ourselves. This Christological move that we are invited to enact is beautifully illustrated in the surreal late-1960s television series *The Prisoner,* a series conceived, co-written by, and starring the late Patrick McGoohan. The show revolves around a secret agent (Patrick McGoohan) who, after resigning under mysterious circumstances, is kidnapped and taken to a strange unknown location. The Village, as it is called, is an elaborate prison that looks to all intents and purposes like a picturesque seaside town. Everyone in The Village is referred to by a number that has been assigned by the authorities. The secret agent is given the number "Six."

The opening credits of each episode involve the following dialogue unfolding between Number Six and the latest Number Two, an authority figure in The Village who is second only to the elusive Number One.

> NUMBER SIX: "Where am I?"
> NUMBER TWO: "In The Village."
> NUMBER SIX: "What do you want?"
> NUMBER TWO: "Information."
> NUMBER SIX: "Whose side are you on?"
> NUMBER TWO: "That would be telling . . . We want information. Information! INFORMATION!"
> NUMBER SIX: "You won't get it."
> NUMBER TWO: "By hook or by crook, we will."
> NUMBER SIX: "Who are you?"
> NUMBER TWO: "The new Number Two."
> NUMBER SIX: "Who is Number One?"
> NUMBER TWO: "You are Number Six."

Number Six has been brought to The Village because those in charge want to know why he resigned. Each episode thus revolves around the ever-escalating conflict between the British agent and his captors. Number Six constantly attempts to escape his bizarre prison, undermine those in power, and find out who ultimately runs The Village, while his captors devise ever more elaborate schemes to break him and extract the information they desire.

The result is a tense psychological drama that explores the nature of power and resistance in contemporary society. On the surface, The Village is a place of freedom and contentment. All one's needs are provided for, and the powers that be appear benign. Yet the calm and free nature of The Village has a deeply uncanny texture—beneath the surface there is constant indoctrination, escape seems impossible, and obscure psychological techniques are routinely employed to keep people docile and obedient.

In addition to this, it is never clear who the prisoners are and who the guards are. In fact, it is unclear as to whether the guards themselves are prisoners. One of the few authority figures we do see (Number Two) changes constantly and would seem to be just as trapped in The Village as everyone else (for instance, Number Two is always terrified when his mysterious superior phones to ask about progress).

Throughout the series Number Six is constantly striving to find out who the power behind Number Two really is. As the dialogue over the credits shows, he is obsessively attempting to unmask the always elusive Number One.

The Prisoner constructs a universe in which there is balance and order, where everything has its rightful place and where everyone fits into the organic whole. This is the same universe that we find in *Star Wars;* however, the former locates the viewer in a fundamentally different position. Both *The Prisoner* and *Star Wars* express a pagan universe—that is, a universe in which there is order, balance, and a clear sense of destiny. However, while *The Prisoner* questions this universe and seeks to break it open, *Star Wars* revolves around the attempt to re-establish the pagan order that is under threat. *The Prisoner* is written from a Christological perspective rather than a pagan one. Here the hero constantly seeks to disrupt the balanced order with a hysterical questioning that threatens to destroy the system (rather than maintain it). From the perspective of the hero, the freedom of the people is really a thinly veiled form of slavery.

What is most fascinating about *The Prisoner* is the eventual discovery of who runs The Village, i.e., the identity of Number One. The frustrating cat-and-mouse game that constantly plays out between Number Six and Number Two as the former tries to find out who is in control is only resolved in the final episode when we are finally confronted with the truth. The answer that we get is truly remarkable and goes far beyond the usual tired suspects, such as the Russians, Vietnamese, Islamic terrorists, big business, our own government, etc. The answer as to who runs The Village has been hidden in plain sight from the very beginning, expressed covertly in the opening credits of each and every episode:

> NUMBER SIX: "Who are you?"
> NUMBER TWO: "The new Number Two."
> NUMBER SIX: "Who is Number One?"
> NUMBER TWO: "*You are,* Number Six."

In short, what the series reveals is that the oppressive power behind The Village is none other than Number Six himself.

He is responsible for this oppressive regime that holds him captive. *He* enables it to function. *He* has built this prison in which he languishes. *He* is the power against whom he rails so passionately.

In *The Prisoner* we are confronted with the idea that it is we who create the Big Other that controls us. While we may experience this Other as separate from us, existing independently of us, and bearing down on us, it is nonetheless our own creation.

We are oppressed by a foreign power that is our own.

We are Number Six and Number One, oppressor and the one being oppressed.

We are a divided subject at war with that which we create and which creates us.

We are alienated from that which is a part of us, that which gave birth to us and grounds us. It is a part of our very essence.

When we are ripped away from the political, social, and spiritual structures that define us, we are really being ripped away from that which we help sustain, that which is both a part of us and bears down on us. The deus ex machina is an idol of our creation. And when we strike at it, we strike at ourselves.

Is this not what we see taking place on the Cross? As Christ is cut off from his own essence, so our loss of the religious God is not the loss of some foreign power external to ourselves, but instead a loss of that which is fully us. When we truly participate in the event of the Cross, we (as Number Six) are forsaken by ourselves (cut off from Number One)—we are cut off from the system that we construct and which constructs us.

Unless You Hate Your Family

When one participates in this death, the result is often dramatic. In the aftermath, people have destroyed possessions, left high-paying jobs, and turned their backs on ingrained habits. Indeed, in my own life, there were three significant acts that resulted from this event that occurred in my late teens. I remember vividly returning home and removing all the possessions from my room; I resolved to stop attending the course I was taking in Computer Studies at an Institute for Further Education; and I informed my parents that I was no longer part of the family.

It is easy to regret such actions as naïve, hurtful to others, and destructive, as they were; and yet, beneath these naïve acts, something profound in my life was unfolding. Each of these acts was the spontaneous, material expression of an inner transformation that had taken place. What happened could not accurately be called an experience, as it was more primal than that. *It was an event that transformed the way I experienced everything.*

As a teenager I did not possess much of real value, my possessions being mostly reflections of what I one day aspired to have or be. Throwing these objects away was simply the working out of the fact that these once omnipotent aspirations no longer held any operative power. This was not some act of protest against my previous life but a spontaneous expression of the impotency of these ideas to mold and direct me. They no longer meant anything.

My course in Computer Studies represented the type of future

I once desired, but now, in the aftermath of my Crucifixion experience, I was cut loose from the pull of this imagined future. I no longer felt constrained to follow the course that had previously seemed the natural thing to do.

And when I confronted my parents with the shocking proclamation that I was no longer part of the family, the words were a clumsy and hurtful way of expressing how the values that had nurtured me from birth no longer constrained me in the way that they had done before—while these values were noble and healthy, they no longer defined the scope and limitations of my existence. This was not some attack on a past that I resented. My upbringing had been a healthy and happy one. The claim was a poorly honed way of expressing the psychological truth that I was now experiencing the future in a radically open way. I was undergoing what Paul wrote of when he noted how Christianity is that which fundamentally breaks with the identities that once defined us.

In order to understand why this breaking away involved a cut against the very ones who loved me most, we must remember that it is the family where we receive our primary socialization. As such it is the place that most influences how we see the world, who we will become, and the place we will take in society. For good or bad, our parents ground us and provide the lens through which we perceive our surroundings.

It is worth considering here Nietzsche's claim that the person of knowledge must be able not only to love her enemies, but also to hate her friends.[7] Something that resonates with what we read in the Gospel according to Luke, who records Jesus as saying, "If anyone comes to me and does not hate his father and mother, his wife and children, his brothers and sisters—yes, even his own life—he cannot be my disciple." [8]

This claim can seem bizarre and out of place in the Gospels, and many have sought to downplay its power or ignore it entirely. However, we must remember that, even more so than today, it was the family in Jesus' time that dictated the scope and limitations of what one would become. The family unit was the place where one gained one's identity, where one learned who was a friend and who was an enemy, who to speak to and who to avoid. In this way the family defined—and still does define—the very contours of one's existence.

In the Christian experience, as marked by the Crucifixion, an imbalance is introduced into this closed system. A sword is forged from the fires of the Crucifixion that breaks these bonds. Because we construct our identity within the family, when we come to cut against that identity, we not only cut against ourselves but also those who formed us. This is not unlike the period in adolescence when teenagers come to deeply question the world of their parents, a world that up until that time has been accepted as scripture.

Is this not what we see fleshed out on the Cross itself? For here we see that separation takes place between Christ and his Father. As the philosopher Slavoj Žižek points out: *"On the Cross Christ shows us what this hatred of one's Father looks like."*[9]

In the undergoing of this Crucifixion event, the previous balance and direction of our lives is fundamentally disrupted. This moment where we lose our identity is one of pure subtraction. It is a moment of radical loss in which all that grounds us dissolves away. All that once nurtured us is lost, and we are left naked and alone.

Here, then, the Christ we encounter on the Cross comes to resemble the sage spoken of in the opening parable, for as we enter into the event of Crucifixion, we experience the loss of all that once gave us comfort and meaning. With Christ we cry out, "Why have you forsaken me?"

CHAPTER THREE

"I'm Not Religious" and Other Religious Sayings

Up in heaven, God watched as a huge fundamentalist conference was put on in His name. Hundreds of people were working round the clock to ensure that everything would run smoothly. When the conference began, God listened to the contemporary rock worship, the passionate sermons, and the booming prayers. He watched all the altar calls and kept a close watch as thousands were slain in the Spirit, spoke in tongues, received healing, and gave rousing prophecies from the pulpit.

But God was insecure and wanted to know if the people involved were really sincere. So, on the last day, He decided to visit in disguise. That morning He slipped into the back of the gigantic conference hall and, during the course of the evening, got talking to one of the stewards volunteering at the event. They hit it off so well that the steward invited him to an afterparty with all the organizers.

At the party God leaned over to the steward and said, "Listen, I am just passing through here, so you can be honest with me. Do you really believe in all this stuff?"

The steward immediately became uncomfortable and replied, "Ssshhh. Don't ask that. Not here. The organizers can hear us."

When God pushed the issue, the steward looked around and saw the worship band, the presenters, and the main speaker, all within earshot. So he whispered, "I can't answer that here, people are listening. Tell you what, meet me at midnight in the car park if you really want to know."

Later that night God went to the car park to meet the steward away from anyone who might overhear.

"Okay," said God, "I have to know. It's obvious you couldn't tell the truth while everyone was listening. So what's the story? Do you not really believe?"

In response the steward looked surprised and declared, "No, no—I have to conceal the fact that I do!"

I'm Not Religious: I Just Follow God

It is not difficult to find the intellectual affirmation of doubt and unknowing within the church today. Many believers explicitly reject the use of God as a solution to some problem. They affirm that a life of faith transcends mere dogmatic affirmations and that it involves an ongoing transformation by love, in love, toward love. They view doubt, ambiguity, and complexity as important aspects of a mature Christianity, they see the experience of God's absence as part of faith, they talk openly about the importance of doubt, and they reclaim parts of their Jewish heritage, a tradition that has always understood faith to be deeper than some mere intellectual assent. One does not need to look far to hear statements like, "I'm spiritual but not religious," or, "I'm not religious, I just follow God." These are statements that reflect the person's belief that they do not reduce God to a concept clumsily used to get through life, justify their actions, and explain the otherwise inexplicable.

To a greater or lesser extent, most contemporary believers are likely to stand with Bonhoeffer in his rejection of the God of religion as unChristian. And they will happily stand shoulder to shoulder with mystics like Meister Eckhart—who condemned the way we treat God like a farmer treats a cow, needing it only for the milk that it produces.[1]

And yet this approach to the divine has so many immediate benefits. Such an understanding of God allows us to escape the difficult job of facing up to life's uncertainties and helps us to justify our mythologies that tell us everything is going to work out fine in the end.

Because of all the psychological benefits, we are reluctant to give this God of religion up, and yet we also wish to step into the truth that Christianity embraces our human condition and asks us to fully experience it. While one might initially think that we can resolve this conflict only by choosing to accept or reject the deus ex machina view of God, we have much more ingenious methods of ensuring that we can both have our cake and eat it too.

Thinking of God as a deux ex machina is so natural for us that we must be wary of those who boldly claim to have left this religious notion behind them. We must look for the wounds that such an event leaves, the marks that we carry with us in the aftermath of our participation in the Crucifixion. The God affirmed in religion is not so easy to walk away from because, like alcohol, this working hypothesis helps us avoid a full confrontation with our lives. While we may want to reject the idea that God is some deus ex machina, we will still want to treat God in this way. And so we must ignore what we claim with our lips and look carefully at our bodies to see if we really do bear the marks of Crucifixion, or if we are simply pretending to ourselves.

In order to understand how we can fool ourselves into thinking that we fully embrace the Crucifixion while avoiding it in reality, it is important to grasp how humans are able to affirm one thing consciously while affirming the opposite thing in the way they live. Or, more precisely, how we are able to affirm one thing consciously *so as to continue to affirm the opposite thing in the way we live*. To understand this let's turn to an insightful anecdote that the philosopher Slavoj Žižek is fond of telling:

There was a young man who met with a psychotherapist once a week for years because he was convinced that he was a seed. Eventually, after many years, he became convinced that he was really a human being. Thanking the therapist, he returned home happy.

However, two weeks later the therapist hears a loud banging on his door. When he opens it, he sees the man back again, sweating and breathing heavily.

"You have to help me," says the man, "my next door neighbors recently bought chickens, and I am terrified that they are going to eat me."

"But surely you know now that you are a human being and not a seed," replies the therapist.

"I know that," he says, "but do the chickens know?"[2]

This bizarre and irrational story contains a profound insight into the nature of belief. It helps expose the logic that enables us to continue to act in a way that we consciously do not see.

Many of us would agree that having a better car, a nicer home, or more possessions will not really make us happier. We are all able to concur that such things are not worth giving too much attention to and that we should not let our relationships suffer in order to achieve them. The problem, however, is that we often walk away from such conversations and *act* as if we do believe they will make us happier and that making our relationships suffer in the pursuit of them is worth it. While we are very quick to say that we do not believe, we continue to act as if we do.

Why?

Because it is not our beliefs that provide the power here, but rather the beliefs bearing down on us from others. It is the beliefs of the magazines and television advertisements that hold the operative power, beliefs that we have internalized but refused to acknowledge. We continue to believe through the unconscious affirmation of the others' beliefs, thus allowing ourselves to reject, ridicule, and renounce the very things that continue to dictate our material actions.

In Žižek's story, the man does not overcome his problem because the analyst spent his time trying to convince the man that he was not a seed, when he should have been trying to convince the *chickens* (which means changing the man's perception of what the chickens think).

We can see this logic play out in an example based on actual clinical observation. A woman sees a counselor because she feels depressed but can't explain why. She finds herself unable to go for job promotions, make new friends, or pursue her passions. When asked directly about her self-image, the woman's responses show that she doesn't have any problems with low self-esteem. And yet it is obvious that she acts in a way that would imply the very opposite. Over time, however, it becomes clear that she believes *her parents* possess a low opinion of her. While she has a healthy, positive image of herself, it is actually the view she has of her parents' perception that holds the operative power.

Or imagine a little boy who is undergoing therapy. When asked directly if he loves his father, the child replies, "Yes." But when asked what his teddy bear thinks, we find that the bear does not like his father at all but is deeply afraid of him. In this way, the child is able to maintain a positive belief in his love for his father while, through the belief of the teddy, expressing his fears. The therapist thus needs to spend time talking to the bear in order to make progress.

The Church as Safety Blanket

In a structurally similar way, believers are able to intellectually espouse the existential doubt, unknowing, and forsakenness found on the Cross by outsourcing their unwavering belief to the chickens: the chickens being, most often, the Church structure itself (the preaching, prayers, liturgies, hymns). This enables us to say that we embrace the reality of doubt and see the value of acknowledging the sense of God's absence while actually protecting ourselves from the psychological impact of these experiences.

Our doubt, while affirmed as genuine, is thus merely intellectual and not something that is entered into. In other words, while believers may say that we turn away from the view of God that simply helps them feel secure, this idea is still enthroned in their liturgical practice and thus remains firmly in place. Only now the God of religion operates in a masked and opaque form.

If we truly seek to experience the psychological effect of the Crucifixion, then we need to "convince" the structures to doubt. If our structures were to invite us into the experience of unknowing and divine absence, we would be more likely to experience it rather than merely pay lip service to it. However, we are protected from this experience as long as the worship songs we sing, the sermons we listen to, and the liturgies we repeat unwaveringly support a religious worldview. We are able to talk passionately about the dark night of the soul without feeling it as long as the worship songs are full of light, the sermons lay bare all mysteries, and the prayers treat God as an object there to tell us it's all going to be OK.

The institution treats God as a cow on our behalf. The worship songs affirm certainty so that we are free to celebrate uncertainty; the sermons relay absolute conviction so that we can freely confess our doubt; and our prayers never question the God of religion so that we can express our cynicism. The structure acts as a security blanket that enables us to speak of the Crucifixion without ever undergoing its true liberating horror.

To gain a better understanding of how this works, let us imagine a child with some kind of comforter walking into a room full of adults. While the child is fully aware that the room is packed with strangers, he does not feel the fear that this knowledge would otherwise provoke within him. When the comforter is removed, the child does not suddenly gain some additional information about the situation. He does not understand something that was previously withheld from him. But he now experiences the fear that naturally arises within a child when he is in a room full of people he does not know. The security blanket enables the child to consciously accept a situation *without experiencing the psychological horror of it.*

The security blanket is not the problem but rather the solution to a problem. It is a way for the child to cope in a situation that would otherwise prove overwhelming. As such it is not in itself a bad thing. However, if the child is not weaned off the security blanket, then he will remain in a state of immaturity and find it difficult to function in social situations as he grows.

Anything can act as a security blanket. For instance, an old picture of a lost love can prevent someone from experiencing the pain that should naturally accompany such a loss. Its role as a security blanket only becomes clear, however, when the picture is lost—for only then does the person break down. The picture thus acts as a psychological crutch that prevents the person from fully confronting the pain of the loss.

In relation to the Church, let us imagine a worship leader coming in one Sunday and performing songs that express doubt, anger, and a sense of divine abandonment. In a healthy congregation, people would be able to enter into the honesty expressed in the music, allowing it to bring them into closer proximity with the reality of the Cross. However, if it were to evoke a deep anxiety in the congregation, then we glimpse how the regular worship at the Church is acting as a security blanket, protecting the congregation from a psychological confrontation with the Cross.

The interesting thing is that many of those who are disturbed by the music may well freely confess to seeing the sentiments expressed as part of an honest, authentic Christian faith. The issue is that they have simply never really experienced the trauma of these ideas until they hear them expressed in the context of the liturgical hour, and it proves too much.

By allowing the Church to believe on our behalf, we are able to say that we don't treat God as a farmer treats his cow—while gaining all the psychological pleasure that results from actually doing so. We thus remain firmly embedded in a religious worldview while denying it.

I Am Not a Fundamentalist; the Structure Is Fundamentalist on My Behalf

It is perfectly possible to imagine a Church in which every single individual personally rejects the religious view of God while being protected from the psychological impact of this rejection through the rituals and liturgical practice they engage in: affirming the power of the deus ex machina, not through their words, but through commitment to certain concrete practices.

The religious approach to faith has thus not been cracked open to reveal a more grounded and Christ-like faith, but rather has simply found a deeper bedrock to cling to. In so much of the contemporary Church, the last bastion of religion is to be found not in people's direct beliefs but rather in the *structure itself*, a structure that continues to admit of no unknowing, doubt, or experience of divine absence. As long as the worship songs we sing, the sermons we listen to, and the liturgies we repeat are kept in the dark and continues to affirm an infantile faith, then we can pretend to ourselves that we are mature and thoughtful. We can affirm the Crucifixion without having to feel it. In short, the institution treats God as deus ex machina on our behalf.

This enables us to ridicule the religious view of God intellectually while affirming this God in our practice and feeling the subjective power of it. The embrace of doubt thus masks the way that our actual practice (Church life, prayers, worship, daily activity) continues to deny it.

What we witness, then, is the rise of a new kind of fundamentalism, one that is rarely noticed or talked about. This is a disavowed fundamentalism, a fundamentalism that continues to operate in the very place where it is directly ridiculed and rejected. In fact, it maintains its operative power through the very gesture of rejecting it intellectually. As the old adage goes, the greatest trick the devil ever pulled was convincing the world he didn't exist.

This is an approach to Christianity that stands as the polar opposite of what we find expressed in the Crucifixion, for on the Cross, religious belief is not *intellectually questioned* ("My God, My God"), it is *robbed of its grounding power* ("why have you forsaken me").

I remember seeing this disavowed form of religious adherence play out while visiting a church nestled in the very heart of New York City. The sermon that week was on the passage in Genesis that describes Jacob wrestling with God. The text in question was used persuasively to explore the reality that we all wrestle with God. The minister who gave the address freely admitted that we all wrestle in our faith and that we all have our doubts. He even affirmed that this is an important part of what it meant to be a Christian. But the message did not end there: The second part of the sermon went on to proclaim that while we may doubt God, we can be confident that God never doubts us. The climax of the sermon came when the preacher claimed that while we may lose our grip on God, we are forever held in the grip of God.

Here we witness a particularly potent expression of how the structure believes for us. For in this vivid sermon we are brought to the brink, to the point where we can almost taste the sweat and tears of Christ as he cries out on the cross; yet, at the last moment, we are pulled back from the precipice. While we are told that it is fine to doubt and struggle with our faith, in the same breath the preacher was able to perform a sleight of hand that enables him to relocate certainty at a higher, hidden level. Our mythologies are thus re-established. The full message here is simple: *We can doubt precisely because of our certainty.* The minister was thus informing us that we could have a dark night of the soul while keeping all the lights on.

I'm Not Religious; I Reject God

At this point someone may wish to point out that while a religious spirit might continue to play out within much of the concretely existing Church, more and more people are turning their backs on this institution. So even if a religious type of Christianity is still prevalent, such an approach to life is on the decrease. However, once more the issue might be more interesting and complex than it first appears.

For instance, there is an interesting phenomenon in which people who have previously rejected their faith return to it as adults. More than this, they often go on to consider their past exploits as a form of backsliding, the result of having fallen away from "the truth." This usually happens when people are faced with something difficult, when they enter into a different stage of life, or when they get older and face the reality of their finitude. At these times they return to the faith they once held, often to the same kind of church they had previously attended, taking up many of the same beliefs.

In these situations, it is clear that the rejection of religion was in no way a signal that people had moved beyond it; their religious commitments were simply lying dormant. They had not gotten to a point where they could live without religion, fully embracing existence without recourse to the God of religion; they had simply entered a time in their life where the direct embrace of religion was not immediately required.

Such people are the most prone to the efforts of evangelical missions, for while it might seem that these individuals have rejected their religion, it is really just lurking beneath the surface, waiting to be sparked back into life. With the right mix of fear and desire, such people can easily be brought back into the fold. For beneath their seeming rejection of everything that previously defined them, they remain fundamentally wedded to their old beliefs. This phenomenon is so common that there is even a popular phrase to describe it, one that originated during the Second World War: "There are no atheists in foxholes." In other words, when there is an enemy to fear, an economic recession to resist, or a disease to face, people who say that they have no religion often find themselves running back to the institution they once ridiculed.

Often this return is stalled by our inability to face up to the difficult situations we are immersed in. To understand how this works, let us compare real world physics to what is called "cartoon physics."

A great scientist (like a great director, writer, thinker, etc.) often lives in deep awe of what the rest of us do not see. The scientist is fascinated by minute realities that we participate in everyday without noticing. Newton was struck by the way objects were attracted to the ground; Darwin was fascinated by the way animals were so well adapted to their environment; and Galileo was obsessed with the movement of the stars. All of these were such simple phenomena to observe and reflect upon that it took some of the world's greatest thinkers to actually do it.

Such study continues to open up a wealth of understanding about the nature of the universe—understanding that has been cashed out in the technological developments we have witnessed since the Enlightenment.

Physical laws would appear to be universal in nature (being the same in any place at any time). And yet, at least in the world of cartoons, they begin to break down. For instance: an anvil will always fall at a slower rate than that of a self-conscious being. More than this, its downward trajectory will always be directly influenced by the location of any character falling past it (invariably landing on them).

In much the same way that the natural scientists discovered great truths by delving into the inner workings of the phenomena that surrounded them, so can we benefit from delving into the world of cartoon physics. Someone might respond by saying that cartoon physics is purely arbitrary—but this is not the case. If what we watch on a cartoon does not strike us as convincing at some level, it won't stand the test of time. Imagine that an anvil, instead of always falling slower than a self-conscious being, always stopped in mid-air. This would make no intuitive sense and would thus provide no pleasure for us.

One of the laws in cartoon physics is that self-conscious beings will not fall until they look down. So what can this tell us? It reflects something of our inner experience. Often we can be pretty sure that we have run off a cliff (being in a loveless marriage, having an undiagnosed health issue, etc.), yet we continue as if we are still on solid ground. We act as if everything is fine and keep up with our daily chores, even though we know we are in trouble. In such situations, we get a horrible feeling that we are about to plummet, yet we do not. It is only as we look down (admit to the lack of love, go to the doctor) that the fall occurs.

It is only when we actually look down that we panic and return to the religious institution, preferring to grab hold of the security blanket it offers rather than undergo the crash. Yet, painful as this can be, the fall is better than the alternative of constantly avoiding it and pretending everything is fine. After enough time has passed, the fall can come as a welcome relief, even in the midst of its pain. Perhaps the good news hinted at in cartoons is that there is life after the fall (although the idea that we will again repeat the whole process that we witness in cartoons is less comforting).

I'm Not Religious; I Don't Even Believe in God

Lastly we have what is perhaps the most interesting form that religiosity takes today. It is a form that can be found among many in the West who take pride in not believing in any ultimate meaning whatsoever. Those who happily affirm only the immanent play of contingency over any notion of a divine plan.

In this situation, people often continue to get the benefit of a belief they do not affirm in much the same way as the parent of a young child gets the benefit of believing in Santa Claus. When as children, we stopped believing in Santa Claus, we most likely experienced a profound sense of disillusionment and sadness. Christmas was drained of all its magic and wonder. However, to the parent of a child, Christmas becomes deeply enchanted once more. While we do not really believe in Santa Claus, we experience all the pleasure and excitement that is directly connected with this belief through the naïve belief of the child. When the child eventually discovers the truth, it is not just the child who faces sadness and disappointment; both child and parent are united in a sense of loss. While one believed and the other did not, both experience the psychological effect of believing. The child's belief enabled the parent to experience the wonder of Christmas again without actually having to believe in it themselves. Hence, when the child stops believing, the parents experience the child's sadness and melancholy. The parents often feel the loss more profoundly than the child.

I remember talking to a parent whose little boy asked if the tooth fairy really existed. She found it very difficult to tell him the truth and experienced a sense of loss in giving the answer. However, upon hearing the truth, the little boy simply asked, "Will I still get my dollar?"

In the same way, we find that there are many who, intellectually speaking, don't believe in any kind of religious (or political) absolute and yet who experience all the comfort and security of such a belief because someone else they are related to continues to believe. It might be that the individual's parents still attend Church (or affirm some political absolute), or a close friend, or someone whom the person looked up to as a child (such as a youth leader or teacher). As long as this other continues to believe, the cynic can have all the intellectual satisfaction of feeling that they are not religious at all without experiencing the pain associated with their cynicism.

It is only when these supposedly liberated, secular individuals hear that the other no longer believes that they feel the pain of the loss themselves. It is only in the other's loss that they experience the psychological effect of what they claim to fully embrace. In this way, the other acts as a security blanket, allowing them to avoid experiencing the pain of what they say they have rejected.

This type of disavowed religiosity is often played out in relation to children. Often parents who have turned away from the Church will still send their sons and daughters to Sunday school and might even return to Church themselves in order to pretend to their children that they believe. Here again the parents can experience the security that comes from religious belief without needing to intellectually assent to it themselves; they can claim that they are not religious at all while still being bound to religion in terms of lived experience. It is only when the child admits to not believing that the parents feel the loss of what they claim not to have.

And so we must be careful not to believe the hype when people claim that religion is declining, whether it is some fiery preacher who is condemning it or a secular humanist who is celebrating it. Religiosity is still embraced by many within the church (who say they aren't religious but simply follow God), by individuals who reject the church (who say that they have nothing to do with the religion of their youth), and by people who ignore the church (saying that religion has nothing to do with them).

Religion as That Which Binds

At this point, fundamentalism might seem to be a more consistent position than what we find in most churches in that the fundamentalists fully confess to be as religious as the structure they participate in. They do not speak of the virtues of doubt while participating in a system that affirms only certainty. They do not affirm the importance of experiencing divine absence while acting as if they are hardwired to the truth. They fully embrace and believe what they practice. However, the reality is quite different.

This is something that we see expressed in the story that opens this chapter, where God attends a fundamentalist conference only to find a participant hiding his full and frank belief. Here we are presented with the idea that those running the conference don't really believe what they profess and seem to live out. The young man to whom God speaks knows his unwavering commitment is something that must be hidden. But what does this mean? Do most fundamentalists really not believe what they say they believe?

To approach an answer, let us take an example that helps to expose how language functions. In Northern Ireland, it is generally polite to turn down the offer of food or drink the first two times it is offered, and only by the third time is it proper to accept. This unwritten rule is not something people are conscious of, but it is an important practice that regulates a ritual of friendship—and it works perfectly until one visits another country. This happened on one occasion while I was visiting Denmark. After a day of traveling, I was hungry and looking forward to some food. When I was offered a local delicacy in someone's house, I of course refused, saying that I wasn't that hungry. But to my surprise, the host simply nodded and took the food away to share with others. I was confused. How rude! In response, all I could say was, "What are you doing? If you want to know whether or not I am really hungry, then why did you simply accept my response that I was not?"

What we learn here is that communication involves both a stated message and a hidden one. This hidden message can be understood only as we glimpse the background network of ideas, customs, and practices that need to remain masked in order for communication to function smoothly. Even the most rigorous discourses (such as what we find in philosophy and science) operate in this way. However, while we all know of these hidden messages, we must act as if we do not know in order for communication to function smoothly.

The more aware we are of how language works, the more difficult it is to use language. In cases of psychosis, the distinction between the manifest message and the hidden message dissolves away, while in neurosis the difference is experienced in too disturbing a way. But, under normal conditions, people operate with this structure continually.

In fundamentalism, we witness a type of psychotic relation to language in that there is an attempt to banish the hidden message from discourse. And yet this proves almost impossible. While everyone in a fundamentalist community may appear to really affirm the religious view of God both intellectually and in Church practice, there is a complex and hidden set of secret messages that tell people when to really believe and when not to. For instance, the claim "God will heal you if you have enough faith" really contains the following secret, disavowed message: "If it's not too serious, pray for it, but if your illness is life-threatening, seek medical help."

The point is that this hidden message can never be admitted in these communities, for the Church rests upon its very denial. To admit to the disavowed messages that operate in the explicit beliefs of the congregation means that one must confess to a form of unbelief unacceptable in fundamentalism.

This distinction between the explicit belief and the implicit true message only really becomes clear when some individual or group (in a truly psychotic fashion) begins to dissolve the difference, something that can have disastrous results.

This is what we see play out in situations like that of Carl and Raylene Worthington, who withheld medical care in 2008 from their daughter because they believed that God would heal her through prayer. The child died of bronchial pneumonia and a blood infection, both of which could have been easily treated with antibiotics. The distinction disintegrated and they really believed what was preached in their church (if you have enough faith God will heal) without taking heed of the coded message embedded in the sermons—if your child is seriously ill, don't waste time praying, but call a doctor.

Fundamentalists thus operate with a structure not unlike that found in more liberal and orthodox traditions; they simply do not acknowledge it as such. The only difference rests in the fact that the doubts they implicitly affirm are not explicitly embraced. Across the various contemporary Christian expressions of faith (conservative, liberal, fundamentalist, evangelical, and orthodox) God is treated as a deus ex machina with all the psychological pleasure that involves. Yet none of these traditions is able to fully live out this belief for any significant amount of time.

What becomes clear as we look at the different ways the deus ex machina operates today is that religiosity is more widespread than most imagine. That religion is not really on the decline, but rather has simply undergone a transformation that makes it harder to identify. Here we also discover something important about the very essence of religion itself—it is not necessarily something we affirm, but rather is a psychological phenomenon. Something hinted at in the very etymology of the word, which has its roots in the idea of binding rather than mere intellectual assent.

This means it is possible for people to believe there is an ultimate meaning in the universe without being religious at all—that is, people do not use this belief in order to avoid a full confrontation with their humanity. It is a belief that they can calmly discuss over a drink and which they are happy to rethink. Such people have a reasoned and healthy belief that does not need to be passionately defended against those who disagree.

It is only if someone holds onto such a belief for dear life, viciously attacking anyone who might threaten it, that we witness a religious attitude at work. Here we see how the belief is required for them to maintain psychological equilibrium.

It is only as we are cut loose from religion in the very depth of our being—experiencing an existential loss of God, rather than some mere intellectual rejection—that we are free to discover a properly Christian expression of faith.

Chapter Four

I Don't Have to Believe;
My Pastor Does That for Me

There was once a British army base located in a tiny town in rural Northern Ireland. The story goes that each time a new battalion of soldiers arrived, one of the resident officers would show them a trick that exposed how dumb the Irish really were.

When the latest group of soldiers arrived, the officer brought them down to the local pub for a drink. When they were settled, he got out an old crumpled five-pound note and a shiny new one-pound coin. As the soldiers watched, he placed them both on the table. Once he had done this, he scanned the bar for one of the oldest and drunkest men in the place and called him over. When the local had settled himself, the officer pointed to the money and said, "I want to give you one of these. Which would you prefer, this bright shiny coin or this old crumpled piece of paper?"

In response the old man picked up the coin, bit into it with his teeth, and exclaimed with delight, "I'll take the shiny gold coin, please."

The soldiers, of course, found this hilarious and started trying it with others in the pub, providing them with endless hours of entertainment.

There also happened to be a tourist in the bar who watched in disbelief what was taking place. When the soldiers finally left, she went up to some of the old men and exclaimed, "Why on earth did you take the coin when you could have had the note? Do you not know that it is worth five times more?"

"Of course we do," replied one of the locals, "but if we took the note, they would stop playing the game."

The Real Job of the Pastor

As we have explored in the previous chapter, the loss of religion is a traumatic experience and one that we often attempt to avoid by using the Church as a security blanket. In this chapter I want to go deeper and explore how this works in relation to the role of church leaders. Previously we saw how the structure itself believes on our behalf, thus protecting us from the experience of doubt, unknowing, and a sense of divine loss. The structure itself is manifest most clearly in the words and actions of those who symbolize the structure, i.e., the pastors, priests, youth leaders, worship bands, and ministry teams. From the last chapter, one might think the way to change the structure is to attempt to convince the people who run the structure that doubt, unknowing, and mystery are all parts of faith and should be expressed liturgically.

However the problem goes much deeper.

Before we touch upon what exactly this is, let us reflect briefly upon an implicit role that Church leaders currently play within the contemporary Church. At its most basic, Church leaders *believe on behalf of the community*. This seems to allow us the freedom to doubt. In this way, the leader, as part of the symbolic structure of the Church itself, protects us from the central experience of Christ on the Cross. The pastor, worship leader, or youth pastor acts as a force field, holding the Christian trauma of the Crucifixion at bay.

If the leader in question speaks of having a sense of deep doubt or shares a current experience of divine loss (rather than something long since past), then that which previously protected us from experiencing our inner darkness is ripped away. Here we are confronted by our own unknowing and must begin to work through the consequences.

In order to participate in the Crucifixion, we must find leaders who openly experience doubt, unknowing, and a deep mystery, leaders who see these as a part of Christian faith and important in our ongoing development of a healthy and properly Christian spirituality. The problem is not that there is a lack of leaders who have these experiences; rather, there is a lack of leaders who can admit to these experiences.

In November 2010, journalist Dan Harris of ABC News explored the subject of ministers who secretly don't believe. As part of his investigation, Harris interviewed two evangelical ministers who spoke articulately about their loss of faith and their inability to speak about the experience, even to those who were closest to them.

The piece itself played on the idea that this was surprising. However, the existence of genuine doubt, uncertainty, and even a total lack of faith among church leaders is a much more common reality than we may initially think. The reason this questioning almost always goes unnoticed is simple: because it so often goes unspoken.

We all know that most pastors doubt and experience a sense of divine absence from time to time, and we know that it is often much more than that. Yet it is evident that they are often unable to express this reality in any public way—at least not unless they immediately follow it up with some safety net claim that God is big enough to contain the doubt (thus expressing an even deeper certainty). On the rare occasion when a pastor does stand up and declare his (or her) embrace of unknowing, a crisis among the congregants can ensue. Not because the congregation now doubts, but because the pastor's belief provided a protective psychological dam that held back their doubt.

Equilibrium is reestablished only when the pastor recants the doubt, is reeducated, or removed. Only when the pastor banishes the doubt or is replaced by someone who can fulfill the role of believer-on-our-behalf, can the church once again act as a metaphysical security blanket, preventing us from experiencing the anxiety of our existence. For any community that has not actively experienced and embraced the forsakenness testified to by the Crucifixion, a pastor who expresses this can prove deeply disconcerting, even inducing anger and despair.

Protect Me from What I Know

Existential crisis generally arises not because of some new information that a person receives, but because they are now confronted with what they already know but refuse to admit. Take the example of popular documentaries dealing with ethical issues. We know that such films, to a greater or lesser extent, effect societal change. When it comes to issues like environmental crisis, animal abuse, persecution of minorities, etc., we can often observe changes in behavior in their aftermath.

But we miss something significant if we think that the change is purely the result of people learning things that they previously didn't know. It is not simply that documentaries such as *An Inconvenient Truth* and *Food Inc.* tell us something that we don't already know. If it were simply a matter of people being exposed to knowledge that they didn't previously have, then there would not be the reality of resistance. Resistance being the response whereby an individual refuses to watch such documentaries (or engage in conversation about the issues they raise) by offering lame excuses, a host of unformulated arguments, and/or showing visible bodily discomfort at the mere suggestion. Such resistance arises as a result of not wanting to be confronted with something that we already suspect might be true.

Of course, there are many things that we are genuinely ignorant about, but by the time a major documentary is released on
some ethical subject, it is usually the case that there is some knowledge about the issues it raises among the general population. So,
while such documentaries may offer us some specific information
that we did not know before, most of the findings will have already
been widely dissipated through various media outlets. We often
change our behavior in light of a documentary dealing with some
ethical issue, not because we are confronted by something we don't
know, but rather because we are confronted with something we already know but refuse to admit to ourselves. When we are directly
confronted by what we know but have refused to admit, we can no
longer pretend that we are ignorant.

What if we already know that our desire for cheap food feeds
gross cruelty and suffering?

What if we are well aware that the way we live is excessive and
that there are ways to consume that minimize our damage to the
planet?

What if we already know that some of the things we desire are
not really worthy of our admiration?

At a basic level, we might wish to pretend to others that we
don't know something that would challenge us to change the way
we live because we don't want them to witness our more callous
nature. However, at a more fundamental level, we often attempt
to pull the wool over our own eyes, pretending to ourselves that
we don't know what we already know. In this situation, we want

to maintain a certain image of ourselves as moral and thus seek to suppress anything that would challenge that image. We may know that there is deep cruelty involved with the dairy industry, for example, but we do not need to admit we know this as long as we are not directly confronted with it.

We can see a manifestation of this refusal to know what one knows playing out on a large scale when, after the Second World War, many civilians in Germany defended their lack of action concerning the mass extermination of Jews by saying that they were not aware of what was happening. While this is no doubt true—in the sense that they would not have known the full facts—there were plenty of hints that something horrific was taking place. There were so many clues that it becomes obvious that many refused to see for fear that they would then need to act. Most of us would have done the same if we had been in their shoes, because it is what most of us do today concerning all kinds of justice.

On the occasions when we are directly confronted with what we know, we have three options: change our behavior, offer embarrassing excuses and caveats that make it obvious we don't really care, or simply admit our lack of concern (which is at least to be respected more than pretending we do care).

In a similar way, when the Christian leader communicates an experience of doubt and divine loss, the congregation can be confronted with what they too believe and yet refuse to fully acknowledge. In order to keep this experience at bay, any personal expression of divine absence is permitted only if it is supplemented by a liturgical structure that obsessively celebrates divine presence and certainty through the music, sermons, prayers, and public beliefs of the leaders.

The admission of divine abandonment is thus robbed of its potency, enabling us to admit that absence and forsakenness are part of our faith without experiencing the transformative trauma of this admission. We are able to look at the Cross from a distance without ever needing to enter into a direct participation with it.

The endless courses on apologetics, triumphalist music, confident prayers, and sermons of certainty don't necessarily reflect the beliefs of the people offering them or receiving them. But everyone participates regardless, because they protect us from facing up to the anxieties of our existence. In this way much of the contemporary Church resembles a drug that prevents us from facing up to the suffering and difficulty that is part of life.

The whole religion industry is thus fueled by our desire to escape suffering and avoid the gnawing sense of meaninglessness. The certainty is marketable because it is a response to our unhappy situation, and it keeps selling because it is ultimately ineffective in properly transforming it. In this way, the religious structure operates in a similar way to how movies functioned during the Great Depression. Despite the poverty, theaters showing musicals, gangster films, and comedies were packed. These films were so popular because they offered people a way of escaping their dire reality for a couple of hours. They offered the audience a way of avoiding their emotional turmoil rather than work through that turmoil.

New Atheism versus Christian A/theism

This structure of certainty is held in place through the combined efforts of all those involved, from those who construct the various liturgical practices to those who participate in them. The result is something akin to the story at the beginning of this chapter—everyone is involved in playing a game that does not reflect what anyone is really thinking. The game does not however require anyone's direct belief in order to function; it simply requires everyone's material participation in it.

The reality is that many well-known worship leaders, youth coordinators, and pastors will, in a private setting, admit to a whole host of questions, doubts, and even disagreements with the theology that they present in public.

There are, of course, considerations concerning how best to express something that people might find difficult, but all too often there is no attempt to express publicly what is being discussed in private. In this way, these private confessions act as a mere release valve that effectively enables individuals to continue performing their public functions, allowing them the intellectual pleasure of admitting their doubts without having to find a way of expressing them within the structure itself—something that we witness in families where the parents secretly have doubts yet never express them to their children, pretending to believe in order to protect them from a sense of anxiety.

One other thing to note about the opening anecdote is the way that the only people naïve enough to take the game seriously are those on the outside, the ones watching on in disbelief at what is transpiring. Does this not represent one of the major drawbacks of the New Atheist movement? Their critique misses the mark by attacking the beliefs of people playing the religious game rather than attacking people's material participation in the game itself. Indeed, some of the major voices in the New Atheist movement express this explicitly when they claim that they have no real problem with people participating in Church life, going on a Sunday to sing and pray, as long as they don't really believe it all. For the radical Christian, however, belief in God, Jesus, and the various claims of the Church are not where the insidious power of religion lies, but rather in one's direct material involvement within a structure that uses these beliefs to protect us from facing the difficulties of life.

In contrast to the New Atheism, the radical Christian affirms what may be called "a/theism." A/theism aims to rupture, not the actual beliefs of a person, but the way those beliefs function as a crutch to prevent the individual from actively participating in the difficult challenge of embracing the world. In short, the critique is not concerned with the content of our mind but is aimed directly at our involvement with a game that many of us do not believe in yet continue to support by our participation.

Creating Structures That Bring Us Face-to-Face with the Experience of Doubt

So then, what would it look like to have a structure that actually invited us to participate in the power of the Crucifixion?

A structure that brought people to the threshold of that loss through liturgical practices that brought us face-to-face with the transforming trauma of Christ's death? Practices designed not to shield us from doubt, but to draw us carefully in? A community that did not protect us from the trauma of forsakenness, but that helped us face it and find life in it?

Such a community would need to ritualize the full range of human emotions, bringing radical doubt, ambiguity, mystery, and complexity into the very heart of the liturgical structure itself. Hymns would need to delve into absence, sermons excavate doubt, and prayers probe the possibility that no one is on the other side. The structure would need to reflect back the experience of Christ on the Cross in such a way as to invite a direct encounter with that event horizon.

In order to understand how this might work, it is worth considering these words of Søren Kierkegaard regarding the nature of a poet:

What is a poet? An unhappy man who hides deep anguish in his heart, but whose lips are so formed that when the sigh and cry pass through them, it sounds like lovely music. . . . And people flock around the poet and say: "Sing again soon"— that is, "May new sufferings torment your soul but your lips be fashioned as before, for the cry would only frighten us, but the music, that is blissful." And the critics come forward and say, "That's the way, that's how the rules of aesthetics say it should be done." Of course a critic resembles a poet to a hair, except he has no anguish in his heart, no music on his lips.[1]

In this poignant reflection Kierkegaard says (under one of his pseudonyms) that a poet is one who suffers on our behalf. If we have encountered the difficulties that are reflected in the lyrics, then we may be gently drawn into the suffering that is expressed in the music, and while we may not necessarily weep, we may find ourselves undergoing the same emotional release that would have taken place if we had. Like the professional mourners who were once paid to attend funerals, so we now pay to attend concerts, read books, watch films, or attend theatrical performances where we may experience an emotional discharge in a way that is cathartic and liberating. In so doing, we participate directly in the suffering and pain reflected in the work, but in a ritualistic manner that does not crush us. This act of mourning thus helps us face up to our suffering and work through it in a healthy way rather than repressing it or being overcome by it. In this way it works in a fundamentally different way from the escapist movies of the Great Depression.

But Kierkegaard notes a second response that one can have to the weeping of the poet—that of the critic. The critic is one who is able to appreciate the music and talk eloquently about the artist's skills and technique, while never entering into the experience that the musician invites us to participate in. The critic is able to comment on the beauty of the music without truly experiencing the trauma that gave birth to it, experiencing it only on the most superficial of levels and maintaining a minimal distance from the emotional impact it might otherwise have. The critic thus never directly touches upon the deep existential truth of the music.

In a similar way, even if the structure itself is able to reflect the experience of Christ on the Cross through its music, sermons, prayer, and ritual, this does not guarantee that one will touch upon that experience. Those for whom the spirit of this event is already brewing will find themselves in a place where they can work through it in a healthy way. But there will always be those who act more like the critic, those who seek to protect themselves by avoiding full emotional involvement in any liturgical practice that seeks to bring us into contact with our pain and suffering. This type of refusal is something that brings us close to what John Wesley called the experience of being "almost Christian."[2] In this state of almost-Christian, nothing is missing in terms of our actual beliefs and practice, nothing is missing but the subjective participation itself.

This idea of truth being manifest only in our participation in it is structurally similar to the experience of love. In the transition from liking someone to falling in love with them, there is the recognition of a previously unseen property in the beloved that transcends all their other traits. The one you love may be attractive, interesting, and creative, but the confession of unconditional devotion cannot arise in response to any of these. Someone may see everything in my beloved that I see, down to the very last detail, and yet not love her. Love involves an act in which one "sees" the other as transcendent, a transcendence that only comes into visibility as we subjectively enter into and intertwine ourselves with the other. When we are presented with the Cross, we may participate in it like a lover or approach it from a distance like the critic who affirms it in every dark detail while remaining distant from its transformative power. While the latter claim to be close in terms of understanding, they are distant in terms of participation. The former however, are distant in terms of understanding (feeling the inherent mystery of the event) and yet stand in utter proximity to it through their experience.

Getting Rid of the Need to Believe

This blowing apart of religion that is testified to in the Crucifixion has nothing whatsoever to do with whether or not someone believes that there is a source for everything that is. As we have already noted, Christ does not intellectually reject the idea of a supreme principle but rather experiences the loss of this belief's comforting power.

We see this idea play out compellingly in the life of Mother Teresa. Mother Teresa first felt a call to become a nun at the age of seventeen and soon after joined an Irish order called the Sisters of Loretto. After training in Dublin and Darjeeling, she moved to Calcutta where she taught geography and catechism at St. Mary's High School. It was, however, in 1946 that she experienced what she termed the "call within the call." Soon after, she left her job as principal of St. Mary's and went to work with the poor and oppressed on the streets of Calcutta. By this time, she was thirty-seven years old. From this time on, she dedicated her whole existence to looking after those who had been given no place within society, serving those who had nothing and who were considered to be nothing. From then on, to her own personal dismay, Mother Teresa quickly became a shining example of what it might look like to embrace the way of Christ.

And yet, in 2007, with the publication of some private correspondence between Mother Teresa and her spiritual directors, people were shocked to find that she lived beneath the shadow of a profound sense of God's absence. For instance, in a letter to Father Joseph Neuner, which is considered to be from April 1961, she wrote,

> Now Father—since [19]49 or 50 this terrible sense of loss—this untold darkness—this loneliness—this continual longing for God—which gives me pain deep down in my heart—Darkness is such that I really do not see—neither with my mind nor with my reason—The place of God in my soul is blank—There is no God in me—When the pain of longing is so great—I just long and long for God—and then it is that I feel—He does not want me—He is not there— . . . God does not want me— Sometimes—I just hear my own heart cry out—"My God" and nothing else comes—The torture and pain I can't explain.[3]

She never stopped believing in God or the central tenets of Christianity. In all of her public addresses and private conversations, she made constant reference to these beliefs. The profound doubt she experienced was existential in nature. She experienced being cut off from God as a living presence standing outside the world and guaranteeing that everything was in order. In this way her life reflected that experience of Christ on the Cross, the cry which addressed God while simultaneously testifying to experiencing the absence of God. In this way her belief was not a security blanket that helped her avoid a confrontation with the experience of unknowing.

Mother Teresa continued to affirm God at an intellectual level, but she passed through the white-hot fires of forsakeness. She is, as such, a shining example of what it means to enter into the fundamental Christian event of Crucifixion.

In short, the Christological crisis is one where everything that grounds us (the political, spiritual, and social) is torn away, where we stare into the void, and, as Nietzsche once said, we feel the void stare back. In this place we are alone as we dimly glimpse life without the gilded cage of religion. And it is here that we stand or fall. Here we must choose whether to embrace life or to turn and run. It is only here, in this dry and barren land of death, that we can approach the truth of life testified to in the event of Resurrection. If, however, Resurrection is not possible, then those who go through this death are, as the apostle Paul knew, "to be pitied more than all men."[4]

Part 2

RESURRECTION

≡

"I am God," says Love.
—MARGUERITE PORETE

For where two or three come together in my name, there am I with them.
—THE WORDS OF JESUS ACCORDING TO THE GOSPEL OF MATTHEW

Chapter Five

Story Crime

There was once a young minister sitting in her house on a Sunday afternoon who was disturbed by a frantic banging on the front door. Upon opening the door, she was confronted by a distraught member of her church. It was obvious that he was exhausted from running to her house and that he was on the verge of tears.

"What's wrong?" asked the minister.

"Please, can you help?" replied the man. "A kind and considerate family in the area is in great trouble. The husband recently lost his job, and the wife cannot work due to health problems. They have three young children to look after, and the man's mother lives with them as she is unwell and needs constant care. They are one day late with the rent, but despite the fact that they have lived there ten years with no problems and will likely have the money later in the week, the landlord is going to kick them all onto the street if they don't pay the full amount by the end of the day."

"That's terrible," said the minister. "Of course we will help. I will go get some money from the Church fund to make up the shortfall. Anyway, how do you know them?"

"Oh," replied the man, "I'm the landlord."

Hiding from Ourselves

To participate in the Crucifixion means to experience a fundamental loss.

On the Cross, God as a psychological crutch dies, and we are overtaken by a deeply felt dark night of the soul. We experience the horrifying sense that life lacks any overarching meaning and the realization that there is no supreme gaze that would ensure our lives have lasting value. At the foot of the Cross, the old religious certainties (be they doctrinal, social, or political) are drained of all operative power, and we are left naked. It is the experience of losing the guiding principle that regulates our time, commands our resources, and dictates our activities. It is the graveyard where religion is buried.

The Cross is the moment when we join with Christ in crying out, "Why have you forsaken me?"

The term "participation in the Crucifixion" thus names the profoundly Christian moment of *undergoing* the death of the deus ex machina. It is where we experience the forsakenness of any absolute paternal figure. To participate in the death of Christ means to be branded by the searing reality of this radical negation.

82

In sharp contrast then to the idea that, at the heart of Christianity, we find the loving embrace of some Supreme Being; to participate in Christ's Crucifixion involves experiencing the destruction of all cosmic security.

Here, in this experience, radical doubt, unknowing, loss, desolation, and forsakenness are to be found.

IT IS PRECISELY THIS experience of the Cross that we seek to avoid in life, for it evokes a terrifying condition called *anxiety*. A condition that is distinct from the experience of fear. Fear is always related to some *thing*, such as an enemy, spiders, or cancer. But anxiety has no object; instead, it is a response to the foreboding shadow of nothingness itself.

The twentieth-century theologian Paul Tillich outlined three distinct types of anxiety, the first two of which we have already touched upon. They are the anxiety of death and of meaninglessness. Each of these is better described as anxiety than fear because both are a response to some kind of lack (the *loss* of life, the *loss* of meaning).

For Tillich, both of these anxieties have a subtle and an aggressive form. The subtle form of the anxiety that arises from a sense of my own end is the feeling that my existence is threatened at a certain point in time (perhaps, for instance, when I narrowly avoid a speeding car). The more aggressive form is manifest when I am directly confronted with the inevitability of my death (perhaps when I find that I have a terminal illness). The more subtle form that the anxiety of meaninglessness takes is the feeling that what I am presently doing has no real value (such as my present job), but it becomes a crushing despair when I sense that everything I could possibly do is without point.

Anxiety is so unnerving that most of us are very adept at protecting ourselves from it, expending a great deal of time and energy ensuring that we never have to confront it. The God of religion is one of the primary ways of protecting ourselves from the onslaught of anxiety and despair. This God enables us to feel that our life is never really under threat and that there is an ultimate purpose to everything.

Another way that we avoid a full confrontation with these anxieties is by avoiding too much self-reflection. We do this by surrounding ourselves with activities that ensure we never have to really be alone with our thoughts. Indeed it is even common for people to discourage too much self-reflection by pointing to the link between thinking and depression. It is thought that too much self-reflection can lead to a dark melancholy. However, what if thinking doesn't make one depressed but rather unveils a depression that had, up until then, gone unnoticed? What if one can be profoundly depressed and yet not even be aware of it?

This is what we see when we observe obsessive behavior such as excessive partying or an unhealthy dedication to one's job. These can often be activities designed to mask a psychological truth too difficult for us to confront—a reality that can also be covered over by activities that are morally commendable, such as spending all our free time working with the poor or dedicating ourselves to politically just causes. However, depression cannot be totally avoided in this way and will find ways of bubbling to the surface in some indirect expression (as a symptom).

It was Freud who pointed out how we can never really escape these anxieties, that what we repress by day will haunt us by night. At its most literal, this means that what we seek to repress in our waking life finds a way to manifest itself as we sleep.

Initially it was recognized that dreams enabled us to extend the duration of our sleep—for we all know that dreams enable us to integrate external distractions such as the sound of an alarm (which might appear in our dream as a phone ringing) or a dog licking our face (which could be integrated into our dream as a kiss).

And yet many of us will, from time to time, experience a more shocking and unnerving side to dreams: those times when we are so disturbed by what we confront in our sleeping state that we jolt ourselves awake. What we can learn from this experience is that sometimes we can have a dream that brings us face to face with the things we would like to repress, a dream that reminds us of something we would rather have forgotten. Perhaps, for instance, it brings to mind a time when someone abandoned us, or when we hurt someone deeply in pursuit of our own pleasure. Here we can experience a profound desire to escape our dream, to flee from what it means by waking up.

One of the twentieth century's towering thinkers, Jacques Lacan, provides a brilliant example of this escape into reality when he describes a dream Freud recorded. A man falls asleep while keeping guard over his son's coffin in an adjacent room. In his dream, the man is confronted by his son, who proclaims, in an anguished voice, "Father, can't you see that I am burning?" At this point the man, who feels a profound guilt over the death of his son, wakes up to a smell of smoke and discovers that a candle has fallen over in the room next door, setting the coffin alight.

The dream itself was no doubt influenced by the smell of smoke, and so the standard explanation for why he awoke is that the smell could not be fully integrated into the dream-state, and thus he was brought back to consciousness. However Lacan posits another possibility, namely that the dream itself was actually inspired by the smell of smoke and resulted in the father's direct confrontation with his guilt: an experience that was so horrific, he sought to escape the dream by waking up. Commenting on this, Žižek writes,

> So it was not the intrusion of the signal from external reality that awakened the unfortunate father, but the unbearably traumatic character of what he encountered in the dream— insofar as "dreaming" means fantasizing in order to avoid confronting the Real, the father literally awakened so that he could go on dreaming. The scenario was the following one: When his sleep was disturbed by the smoke, the father quickly constructed a dream which incorporated the disturbing element (smoke-fire) in order to prolong his sleep; however, what he confronted in the dream was a trauma (of his responsibility for the son's death) much stronger than reality, so he awakened into reality in order to avoid the Real.[1]

In this way we learn that what makes up our waking life (jobs, leisure activities, etc.) can act as a protective screen that shields us from a direct encounter with what really matters to us. Here we can understand what Lacan means when he claims that truth has the structure of a fiction. For it is in the "fiction" of the nightmare that we confront the terrible truth of what drives us.

This can help us to understand why so many of us can find it difficult to sleep. For in our dreams we can encounter ourselves in a way that we protect ourselves from during the day. This is why obsessive late-night partying, drinking, drug-taking, and socializing are not necessarily to be interpreted as attempts to make mundane reality more interesting and exciting. Rather they are often futile strategies to ward off the horrifying Real that awaits us in our dreams and moments of reflection.

On Avoiding the Truth of Who We Are

In addition to death and meaninglessness, there is a third anxiety that Tillich writes of: guilt. Again, this has its weak and strong manifestations. In its weakest form, we have the sense that we have done something wrong in a particular situation. In its strongest form, we feel that we are fundamentally flawed at the very core of our being. And just as we try to avoid facing up to our fears of death and meaninglessness, so too we attempt to cover over our profound sense of guilt.

The main way that we do this is through the embrace of a story that we take to represent the truth of who we are.

We all have a story that we tell ourselves about ourselves, a story which we begin identifying with from infancy, and as long as we don't think too much about it, we are able to maintain this story. But this personal narrative often has little direct connection to the reality of who we are.

Take infamous New York mobster John "Junior" Gotti, who finished a children's book while in prison entitled *The Children of Shaolin Forest*. This stark contrast between his public acts and the writing of a children's book can strike us peculiar. Here we are confronted with someone accused of murder, conspiracy to murder, and armed robbery, who was sitting in a cell, writing a touching and sentimental story for children.

This is not dissimilar to a situation that was well noted in Northern Ireland during The Troubles. At that time it was common knowledge that many of the Loyalist paramilitary leaders had a great sense of humor. They were known to make biting jokes at their own expense and, over a drink, exchange an unending litany of funny, self-deprecating anecdotes. These individuals, when encountered in a social environment, were a lot of fun to be around.

In both these examples, people responsible for terrible atrocities were, when encountered in a more personal setting, experienced as deeply human. When confronted by this, we must ask ourselves what to make of the idea that listening to another person's story helps to turn a stranger or even an enemy into a friend.

Does there not seem to be an inherent limitation built into this saying? Not in terms of it being false, but rather in terms of it being true. What if individuals like Gotti are likable once you have had a chance to really chat with them? What if, under the right circumstances, I really could enjoy the company of some very dangerous individuals? Is it possible that, at a personal level, they are really not all that different from me? They, too, love children, care for their friends, give quietly to charity, tell jokes, share their sufferings over a drink, etc.

It is increasingly popular in the West to focus upon the subjective side of people as the site of an individual's truth. We see this play out in popular culture with the rise of social networking media, where the emphasis is on displaying the more personal sides of our life in a public setting. Now we can "know" public figures at an intimate level through their Twitter updates, personal photographs, and Facebook profiles. We can see that they shop in the same places we do, listen to the same bands, and have similar embarrassing photographs of themselves. More than this, we witness a turn to the subjective on TV and in films, where there is an increasing tendency toward the inner or private world of figures who were once mysterious. For instance, we see TV programs that explore the "behind the scenes" life of vampires, mobsters, and superheroes. In such programs there is a tendency to move the objective practices of the vampire, mobster, or superhero into the background and focus more on the motivations and feelings of the protagonists.

A powerful example of this idea can be seen in the following article from the popular magazine *Homes and Gardens*. The article in question is taken from their November 1938 edition and describes the home and lifestyle of a well-known public figure:

> There is nothing pretentious about the Führer's little estate. It is one that any merchant of Munich or Nuremberg might possess in these lovely hills . . .
>
> Meals are often served on the terrace on little tables shaded by big canvas umbrellas . . . Here Hitler will read the home and foreign papers which his own air pilot, Hansel Baur, brings him every day from Berlin before lunch . . .
>
> Hitler delights in the society of brilliant foreigners, especially painters, musicians and singers. As host, he is a droll raconteur. . . .
>
> The guest bedrooms are hung with old engravings. But more interesting than any of these to the visitor are the Führer's own water-colour sketches. Time was when a hungry Hitler was glad to raise a few marks by selling these little works; none measures more than about eight inches square, and each is signed "A. Hitler"—unmistakably, if also illegibly!
>
> The gardens are laid out simply enough. Lawns at different levels are planted with flowering shrubs as well as roses and other blooms in due season. The Führer, I may add, has a passion about cut flowers in his home, as well as for music.
>
> Every morning at nine he goes out for a talk with the gardeners about their day's work. These men, like the chauffeur and air-pilot, are not so much servants as loyal friends.

A life-long vegetarian at table, Hitler's kitchen plots are both varied and heavy on produce. Even in his meatless diet, Hitler is something of a gourmet. . . . His Bavarian chef . . . contrives an imposing array of vegetarian dishes, savoury and rich, pleasing to the eye as well as to the palate, and all conforming to the dietic standards which Hitler exacts. But at Haus Wachenfeld he keeps a generous table for guests of normal tastes . . .

Elaborate dishes will be served with fine wine and liquors of von Ribbentrop's expert choosing. Cigars and cigarettes are duly lighted at this terrace feast—though Hitler himself never smokes, nor does he take alcohol in any form.

All visitors are shown their host's model kennels, where he breeds magnificent Alsatians. Some of his pedigree pets are allowed the run of the house, especially on days when Herr Hitler gives a "Fun Fair" to the local children. . . . It is then the little ones are invited to the house. Coffee, cakes, fruits and sweets are laid out for them on trestle tables in the grassy orchards. The Frauen Goebbels and Göring, in dainty Bavarian dress, arrange dances and folk-songs while the bolder spirits are given joy-rides in Herr Hitler's private aeroplane. . . .

"This place is mine," he says, simply. "I built it with money that I earned." Then he takes you into his library where you note that quite half of the books are on history, painting, architecture and music. When it is fine enough to dine in the open air, one sees a piano made ready for the after-dinner concert. Local talent will provide violin and cello for pieces by Mozart or Brahms.[2]

What is most troubling about this article is not that it is somehow inaccurate, painting a false image of Hitler's private world. The truly disturbing reality of the article lies in its *accuracy*. Hitler was well known to be a strict vegetarian who avoided alcohol, loved animals, was kind to his staff and enjoyed the company of children. Hitler was likely an interesting person once one got to spend time with him in a more private and intimate setting. This is so difficult for us to accept because we are accustomed to thinking that the truth of a person is discovered best in such a setting.

When confronted by the article above, we are forced to acknowledge the dark underbelly of the popular wisdom that an enemy is simply someone whose story you have not heard. What if this is true? What if most people, at a subjective level, are not that different from us and might actually be people we would enjoy spending time with? Here we must avoid the temptation to be fooled by the subjective story of the other. For what we must remember here is that the truth of a person is to be located, not in the story they tell about themselves, but in the drives and desires that manifest themselves in material practices. The truth of Hitler is not found in the story he tells about himself but in what drove him to such monstrous evils. The article above is exactly the type of story Hitler would have told himself about himself in order to avoid facing up to the disgusting truth of who he was. And, of course, the same is true of Gotti and the Loyalist paramilitaries, whose truth is found in the desires and drives that are manifest in their actions rather than in the fact that they write touching stories for kids or express humor and humanity at the pub.

I Wear a Mask That Looks like Me

The question then is whether the story we tell ourselves about ourselves functions in much the same way. In order to answer that, let us consider the growing phenomenon of online social networking sites.

These sites can be described as offering the world an idealized reflection of ourselves. They express an image of ourselves that we would like other people to believe reflects who we are. Indeed, more fundamentally, they enable us to construct an image of ourselves we would like to believe that we are. On our profiles we list all the films that we want people to think that we like while failing to mention some of the more embarrassing ones, or we post the books that help to solidify a certain image while avoiding our guilty pleasures. More than this we will often only post pictures that make us look good and remove tags from photos that put us in a bad light. For instance, I remember being at MoMA in New York City and overhearing a young girl asking someone to take a picture of her looking at a particular piece of art for her Facebook profile. It was quite obvious that the girl had little interest in the art as such (moving on as soon as the picture had been taken), but she was interested in creating an image of herself as the type of person who would be interested in that particular painting. One could say that she desired to be the type of person who would like that piece of art or, what amounts to almost the same thing, that she would like other people to think that she was the type of person who would like that piece of art.

It would be a mistake, however, to limit our reflections to the rather mundane claim that Facebook tends to reflect an idealized version of our conscious self. We must go deeper and approach Facebook as itself derivative of a more basic psychic structure—the reality that our conscious self is an idealized expression of who we are. *Our conscious self* is the idealized version of ourselves that we present to the world, and our Facebook profile simply reflects that. The significant gap does not then lie between our Facebook profile and our conscious self; rather it rests in the difference between our conscious self (reflected in social networking sites like Facebook) and the truth of who we are.

We hide every day behind a mask that is a Photoshopped version of ourselves.

Take an example of parents going into a supermarket and buying their child some chocolate as a treat. As they are doing this, let us imagine that they notice someone stealing from the same store. They are angered by what they see and tell a security guard who promptly arrests the shoplifter. In this situation we witness the law-abiding parents and the criminal who breaks the law. The problem, however, is that we can fail to look at the situation in its wider context. It is likely that the chocolate bar which the parents bought was made with cocoa beans picked in Ivory Coast by children the same age as their own, children who have no rights, who work inhumane hours, and who suffer continual abuse. Here we can say that while it is clear that there is a law and a crime that transgresses the law, we can miss the way in which the legal system itself, in its failure to intervene in how the chocolate gets to the shops, is itself criminal.

The point here is that the parents can feel rightly moral and just while wholly participating in an immoral and unjust system. (It is one thing if the parents really have no idea about the wider system they participate in, but most of us do have an awareness of these issues but prefer not to confront ourselves with them.)

Maintaining the Gap between Perception and Reality

The process of creating this mask begins at a very early age and is an important aspect of our development. We can see it at work when, for instance, a small boy is running beside his mother. His mother will often hold back and encourage him by saying, "You are such a fast boy." Here the story that the mother is telling the child is a lie. The boy is not really very fast and does not have the ability to outrun his mother. But the story is a useful lie that helps the child to build up some positive self-esteem. It is a story that the child happily takes on and begins to believe.

As we grow, our masks become ever more elaborate and often have little connection with the truth of who we are. These masks enable us to hide the truth of our own desires from our own gaze, something that we see played out in the opening story of the land-lord. The story can catch us off guard because of the way that it expresses a seemingly absurd gap between the landlord's desire to help this struggling family and the fact that it is his very actions that are causing the problem in the first place.

Yet it would be a mistake to think that the twist in the story arises only from the fact that there is a gap between the landlord's desire to help the family and the reality of his actions. After all there, is nothing too surprising about someone struggling between his desire to help others and his desire to make a living. Rather the anecdote derives its counterintuitive power from the fact that the landlord does not experience this gap as a conflict at all. This is not someone who is in conflict with himself—he has found a way of both having his cake and eating it: being able to show deep concern for what is taking place while at the same time profiting from it. He has found a way to maintain the pleasure of being a harsh and unyielding landlord (making money off the family) while simultaneously disavowing the pleasure so as to minimize any guilt (asking the Church to help).

While it would initially seem that this landlord is engaging in a bizarre form of hypocrisy that could only really exist in fiction, the question we must ask is whether this parable actually reflects our daily reality.

Take the example of a little girl being caught by her parents doing something bad and then adamantly proclaiming, "I'm a good girl." The story that the child is telling both herself and her parents attempts to cover over the reality of the situation, helping the child to mask the truth of her actions. The story being told helps to cover over the trauma of facing up to the reality.

This split between what we say and what we do is a direct expression of irony. Something we see at, say, a '70s party, where people dress up in the most flamboyant of clothes and dance to the most idiosyncratic music of the era while simultaneously ridiculing it. Here people laugh at the music they are dancing to and mock the outfits they are wearing. They thus attack the very activity in which they are fully immersed.

In daily life we engage constantly in this ironic gesture. For example, most of us would agree that pursuing wealth at the cost of all else will not make us happier, or that owning a larger home will not make us truly more content, or that working all the hours we possibly can is not the way to get the most out of life. The problem, however, is the way in which we go on acting as if pursing wealth will make us happy, as if owning a larger home will increase our level of contentment, and that working harder will help us get more out of life. Here we disavow the very activity that we are engaged in. We ridicule the ideas that regulate our material existence. We serve an ideology that we intellectually reject.

Irony does not simply describe the gulf that exists between our beliefs and our actions. Rather irony describes the way in which this gulf between our beliefs and practices is maintained through its very denial. Or, to put it another way, irony is the act of masking the gap that exists between our beliefs and actions.

This understanding can help us approach the verse in Matthew that reads,

"No one can serve two masters. Either he will hate the one and love the other, or he will be devoted to the one and despise the other. You cannot serve both God and Money."[3]

When confronted with the idea of dedicating ourselves to the service of love and mercy or to the obsessive accumulation of money at the expense of everything, there are few of us who would choose the latter. Most of us will want to claim that we serve the former. However, the verse refers to the idea of *devotion* rather than *intellectual assent*. Here the point is not what we say we serve but what we are truly devoted to in our everyday existence: What we give our energy, our passion, and our dreams to. In short, what we allow to regulate our existence and resources. Our material commitments will show us which master we love and which we hate; not what we confess in our poetry and prose. In this way, it is often the people around us who will be better at judging what we really love than we ourselves, for we are very adept at hiding from ourselves the truth of our desires.

I Am Hidden in What Is Visible

People's actions can tell us more about their basic drives and desires than the story they tell themselves about themselves. This is what Bonhoeffer was reflecting upon when he wrote in a letter,

> The secrets known to a man's valet—that is, to put it crudely, the range of his intimate life, from prayer to his sexual life— have become the hunting ground of modern pastoral workers.

In that way they resemble (though with quite different inten-
tions) the dirtiest gutter journalists. . . . In a flower garden they
grub around only for the dung on which the flowers grow.[4]

Bonhoeffer is ridiculing the clergy for becoming obsessed with
what people get up to behind closed doors.

To Bonhoeffer, the Bible never makes this distinction between
the inner and outer in the way that we think of it today, but rather
addresses the entire human being. In relation to this he writes,

The "heart" in the biblical sense is not the inner life, but the
whole man in relation to God. But as a man lives just as much
from "outwards" to "inwards" as from "inwards" to "outwards,"
the view that his essential nature can be understood only from
his intimate spiritual background is wholly erroneous.[5]

In short, what we express in our actions is a reflection of what
is within, and vice versa. Yet the story we tell ourselves about ourselves so often masks this. In the Gospel according to Mark we find
a potent example of this self-delusion when Peter vigorously insists
that he would never deny his Messiah:

"You will all fall away," Jesus told them, "for it is written:
"'I will strike the shepherd,
and the sheep will be scattered.'
But after I have risen, I will go ahead of you into Galilee."

Peter declared, "Even if all fall away, I will not."

*"I tell you the truth," Jesus answered, "today—yes, tonight—
before the rooster crows twice you yourself will disown me three
times."*

*But Peter insisted emphatically, "Even if I have to die with
you, I will never disown you." And all the others said the same.*[6]

Here Jesus brings Peter face-to-face with a truth about his life,
yet Peter is unable to accept it—what Jesus says does not match up
with the image he has of himself. Later we read:

*While Peter was below in the courtyard, one of the servant
girls of the high priest came by. When she saw Peter warming
himself, she looked closely at him.*

"You also were with that Nazarene, Jesus," she said.

*But he denied it. "I don't know or understand what you're
talking about," he said, and went out into the entryway.*

*When the servant girl saw him there, she said again to those
standing around, "This fellow is one of them." Again he denied it.*

*After a little while, those standing near said to Peter, "Surely
you are one of them, for you are a Galilean."*

*He began to call down curses on himself, and he swore to
them, "I don't know this man you're talking about."*

*Immediately the rooster crowed the second time. Then Peter
remembered the word Jesus had spoken to him: "Before the
rooster crows twice you will disown me three times." And he
broke down and wept.*[7]

It is then only when he is brought to the place where he is able to reflect upon what he has already done that he is able to see the truth that Jesus spoke.

What drives us is never easy to see. For while it is not hidden within us, neither is it manifest in plain sight. Rather it is *hidden* in plain sight.

This logic is expressed in the joke about a man who crosses a border regularly with a wheelbarrow full of junk. The border guards eventually get a tip off that he is smuggling items over the border. So each time he passes their checkpoint, they stop him, search him and look through the old junk in the wheelbarrow, but they never find anything of interest. Many years later, after he has stopped crossing the border, one of the guards sees him drinking in a bar and approaches, saying, "Come on, we know you were smuggling something all those years, tell me, what was it?" In response the man turns to him and says, "I was smuggling wheelbarrows, of course!"

The point here is that the truth of who we are is hidden in plain sight in much the same way that the evidence of a murder is hidden in a detective novel. In the standard detective story everything is there for us to solve the murder, but while all the evidence is in front of us, it requires great skill and dedication to decode it. This is why we need spiritual disciplines such as prayer, reflection, study, journaling, and counseling. Instead of looking "within" in order to find out what really drives a person, we must look very carefully at the surface itself, decoding what is given and paying heed to the subtle clues that make manifest a person's real desire.

What we begin to realize in all of this is that we are a mystery unto ourselves. Is this not the fundamental problem with the premise of Nancy Meyers's film *What Women Want*? Here the main protagonist, Nick Marshall (Mel Gibson), has an accident that unintentionally gives him the ability to hear the thoughts of women. With this new gift he is supposedly able to work out what women want by listening to their inner monologues. Here the film presents the split between speech and thought as fundamentally significant—it assumes that women know what they want (and, of course, by implication, that men do) and that all we would need to do in order to discover it is to access the others' *thoughts*. However, the question remains as to whether we know what we want; in other words, whether our real desires are to be found in our internal monologues.

Our Practices Do Not Fall Short of Our Beliefs; They Are Our Beliefs

It would be difficult to find a sincere Christian who would wish to attack the idea that Christianity involves the entire person. Throughout the Bible we are confronted with prophets who condemn any expression of faith practice entirely composed of words and rituals. They rail against any practice that is not cashed out in a concern for righteousness and justice, which pays no heed to the widow and the orphan, and which turns a blind eye to the cries of the poor and oppressed.

As a direct result of this, much preaching and teaching is aimed squarely at closing the gap between the verbal affirmation of God and living this out in practice. This teaching claims that it is not enough simply to proclaim a God of love, forgiveness, and compassion without living out the values of love, forgiveness, and compassion. However, behind this worthy desire to close the gap between words and deeds lie three interrelated problems. Let us take each in turn.

First, this attempt still prizes belief over action. Claiming that we should bring our actions into line with our beliefs still places intellectual confession at the center, as that which we must attempt to live up to.

Second, the very act of trying to overcome the divide between what we say we believe and our actions means that this distinction is taken as significant. All the energy that is exerted in attempting to close the gap between what we think and how we act fails to acknowledge that *our practices do not fall short of our beliefs,* but are the concrete, material expression of them. In other words, our outer world is not something that needs to be brought into line with our inner world *but is an expression of it.*

Finally, the very attempt to bring our actions into line with our stated beliefs can actually act as a barrier to transformation.

Paul articulates this reality when he writes of how the law does not stand in opposition to sin but rather is interwoven with it. In other words, the law and sin do not exist at opposite ends of a spectrum but rather occupy the same space and stand opposed to a fundamentally different mode of being (that of love). Here the law is not simply that which forbids sin but also is that which generates and maintains the desire to sin. The prohibition of the law is thus revealed by Paul as that which generates the very desire to transgress the prohibition.

Again let's look at the example of a child: telling a child not to open a door feeds her desire to open the door. The child may be fearful of her parents and thus not actually open the door, but the desire is born in the prohibition, and the more she resists opening the door, the more she will want to do so. This parental command is then internalized, and the conflict between her desire and his parents' desire is relocated in her own being. Here she experiences both the desire to obey and the desire to transgress at one and the same time.

One does not need to look far to see this expressed in preachers who rant against sexual practices they actively engage in, or who speak of generosity while demonstrating greed, or who preach forgiveness while harboring the most violent of attitudes against those who stand opposed to them. Of course one might just say that these individuals are simply hypocrites and insincere. And that is no doubt true of some. But what if many of them are very sincere about what they preach and that their transgression is actually intimately connected with their sincere opposition to that transgression? What if the idea that not all things are permissible, far from being helpful, is the very thing that stops them from finding freedom? And in contrast, what if Paul's radical claim that all things are permissible is the very embodiment of a grace that can actually lead to fundamental change.[8] We can see this idea worked out in the following story:

There was once a young man called Caleb who was obsessed with gathering up possessions and gaining status. He was so driven by the desire to succeed that, from an early age, he managed to become one of the most prominent and influential figures in the city. Yet he was not happy with his lot. He worked long hours, rarely saw his children, and often became irritable at the slightest problem. But more than this, he knew that his lifestyle met with his father's disapproval.

His father had himself been a wealthy and influential man in his youth, but he had found such a life shallow and unsatisfactory. As a result, he had turned away from it in an endeavor to embrace a life of simplicity, fellowship, and meditation.

Caleb's father had taught him from an early age about the problems that come from seeking material and political influence, and he warned Caleb in the strongest possible way to embrace a life that delves deeply into the beauty of creation, the warmth of friendship, and the inspiration derived from deep and sustained reflection.

Caleb's father was an inspiring man, well loved by all, and Caleb could see that his father, while living in a modest way, was at peace with himself and the world in a manner that his friends and colleagues were not. Because of this, Caleb often looked with longing at his father's lifestyle and frequently detested the path that he had personally chosen. Yet, despite this, he was still driven to pursue wealth and power.

It was true that his father was a happy and contented man, but he was also concerned about his son, and on any occasion when they spent time together, he would criticize Caleb for the life he had chosen.

But one day while Caleb's father was reflecting upon his son's life, a voice from heaven interrupted him, saying, "Caleb is also my son, and I love him just the way he is."

Caleb's father began to weep as he realized that all these years he had been hurting his son through his disapproval and criticism. So he immediately visited his son's house and offered a heartfelt apology, saying, "Please never feel that you have to change what you do or who you are. I love you without limit and condition just as you are."

After that day, the father began to take an interest in his son's life again, asking questions about what he was doing and how his work was progressing. But increasingly, Caleb found that he was no longer so interested in working the long hours. Soon he started to skip work in order to spend more time with his family and began to take less interest in what others thought about him.

Eventually, Caleb gave up his work entirely and followed in his father's footsteps, realizing that it was only after his father had accepted him unconditionally for who he was that he was able to change and become who he always wanted to be.

This is nothing less than a description of grace. In grace we are able to accept that we are accepted and, in this very act of knowing we do not have to change, we discover the ability to change. It is in experiencing the license of grace rather than the legalism of prohibition that real transformation becomes possible.

So then we have explored how we seek to avoid facing up to the possibilities that life is finite, our activities are meaningless, and our lives are more dark and selfish than the image we have of ourselves.

We have also seen how we avoid each of these through various distractions, a religious notion of God, and carefully crafted false stories of who we are.

Worst of all, Christianity has become little more than an ideological support of these strategies. The result is a Christianity that (1) offers us various activities to help divert our attention from anxiety, (2) affirms a religious notion of God, and (3) confirms that we are what we say we believe. The life of faith is thus reduced to a crutch, and the Crucifixion becomes nothing more than a mythology we pay lip service to.

The Church in its currently existing form is then an institution that helps us to cover over our anxiety and encourages us to think that faith is lived out in singing songs, engaging in certain rituals, and believing certain things. The Church thus ends up helping us maintain psychological equilibrium and integrate into society as it presently stands rather than throwing us off balance and being a catalyst for the transformation of society.

In this way, we witness the reintegration of paganism into Christianity—Gnosticism—the reintegration of balance and cosmic order into the rupture brought about by Christ. Something that is witnessed in the hymn "All Things Bright and Beautiful," which originally contained the lines,

> *The rich man in his castle,*
> *The poor man at his gate,*
> *God made them, high or lowly,*
> *And ordered their estate.*

Christianity in this hymn is thus presented as a faith that justifies the world as it presently exists. The song implies that the present order is divinely instituted and that we must both celebrate it and protect it.

But what is truly revolutionary about Christianity is the way that it frees us from the power of the religious, Gnostic, God. In our experience of the Crucifixion, we fully confront the anxiety of death, meaninglessness, and guilt that the Church so often attempts to protect us from. A confrontation that must happen if we are to ever enter into the new life described in in the Gospels as Resurrection. For Resurrection life is not some turning away from the experience of death that we find in the event of Crucifixion but rather describes a way of living in its very midst and finding there a way of truly affirming life.

Chapter Six

We Are Destiny

There was once a young novice who set out on a pilgrimage to one of the world's great temples. While on his journey, he stopped at a small village and was given hospitality in the hut of a childless couple. Before the novice set out the next morning, the husband said to him, "You are going to the great temple in the East. Please intercede for us and ask the Lord to bless us with a child."

The novice agreed and, after he had offered the various sacrifices in the temple, said to the Lord, "On my journey a man and his wife were very gracious to me. Please be merciful to them and give them a child."

However, the Lord replied with a heavy heart, saying, "I am truly sorry, but it is not in their destiny to have children." The novice put it out of his head, performed his devotions, and traveled home.

Some years later this novice set out once more on the same pilgrimage and stopped at the same village. Again he was given hospitality by the same couple. This time, however, there were two little children playing at the entrance of the hut.

"Whose children are these?" he asked.

"Mine," replied the man. The novice was intrigued. The man went on, "Soon after you left us, a great saint passed through our village. Like you, we offered him a place to stay for the night. Then, the next morning he blessed my wife and me, and these children are the fruits of that blessing."

When the novice heard this, he could not wait to get to the temple and question the Lord. When he finally arrived, he ran up to the entrance of the temple and shouted, "Did you not tell me that it was not in the destiny of that couple to have children?"

To which the Lord replied, "Yes, that is true."

"But they have two!"

When the Lord heard this, he paused for a moment and then laughed out loud, "Well, that must be the doing of a saint, for they have the power to change destiny!"[1]

Embracing the Night That Embraces Us

To experience the Crucifixion is to lose all the supports that would protect us from a direct confrontation with the world and with ourselves. We are robbed of all the stories that we construct about God and our own nature. Stripped of the guarantees and fantasies that previously marked our existence, we come face-to-face with anxiety in its various manifestations (death, meaninglessness, and guilt). But if this is what it means to experience the Crucifixion, then what can it mean to participate in Resurrection? For the story found in the Gospels does not conclude at the foot of the Cross. Instead the New Testament testifies to a life that overcomes death and invites us to participate in a different reality, a reality called Eternal Life. This phrase can be misleading as it is often claimed to refer to the mere continuation of this life into eternity, but the New Testament writers are clear that they are not speaking of the prolonging of our present life but rather about our entry into an utterly new mode of life, one that starts right here, right now. *Eternal life is thus fundamentally a transformation in the very way that we exist in the present.*

The promise of life in all its fullness (John 10:10) is then something that we are invited to taste in the present moment; it is a depth of being that we can experience now. The shift is so significant that pre-Resurrection life is even spoken of in terms of being a living death (Luke 9:60).

This is not, however, some new mode of living that negates all of our suffering and pain, helping us to escape the world that we live in. Resurrection is not some form of ascension in which we are miraculously transported out of our immediate problems or ripped away from our humanity in all of its frailty. Just as the resurrected Christ is said to have borne the scars of the Crucifixion, so our Resurrection life will continue to bear the marks of the death we had to undergo. This new mode of living is not one in which the anxiety of death, meaninglessness, and guilt are taken away; it is one in which they are robbed of their weight and sting.[2] In this new life, we do not escape our humanity but rather are invited to delve more deeply into it.

From the very beginning, we humans have wanted to escape this world, to become like gods. We have wanted to escape the limits we feel and gain a god's-eye view of the universe. Yet what do we find in the Gospel narratives? We find there the unique idea that God became human and dwelt with us. The desire to escape our humanity and become like God is twisted and turned on its head, throwing us back into our humanity. The Incarnation tell us that if we want to be like God, then we must be courageous enough to fully and unreservedly embrace our humanity.

The biblical understanding of Resurrection is often presented as some kind of answer to the Crucifixion—as some way of return-ing to the God of religion (re-establishing the idea that everything is under control). But instead we must read Resurrection in its full radicality: as the state of being in which one is able to embrace the cold embrace of the Cross. If the Crucifixion marks the moment of darkness, then the Resurrection is the very act of living fully into this darkness and saying "Yes" to it. The faith that is born in Resurrection does not enable us to escape these deeply troubling anxieties; it provides the power to face up to them.

In Crucifixion we are brought to a place in which we feel the full weight of anxiety bearing down upon us without anything that would shield us. It is in light of such debilitating anxiety and the threat of losing oneself in despair that we often cling to religion in its various forms, for religion offers us the tantalizing possibility of escaping the angst that threatens to destroy us. But in the image of Christ, we bear witness to the divine sharing fully in our existence (Incarnation) and offering a way of gaining victory amidst it (Resurrection) through the loss of all that would claim to protect us (Crucifixion). Names like Conversion and Rebirth are given to our participation in this divine movement that takes us from Crucifixion into Resurrection. Conversion is a term that hints at the possibility of a life that is possible *before* death, a life freed from repression and despair. This type of life *before* death is one in which we are able to fully embrace and affirm our existence in the very midst of all that would threaten to destroy it.

Giving Up the World to Find God

When we are caught in the religious worldview, we are torn between two equally unappealing realities. Our existence is either one in which we have to renounce our true object of desire as impossible to grasp, or we pursue it relentlessly and become burned out. Here God is not to be found in this world, except perhaps in hints and elusive moments of grace. Hence, while we get on with life as best we can, this is really a waiting room where we ready ourselves for the next life. Nothing in this world can offer any sustainable satisfaction, and so we are condemned to a type of half-life.

An extreme version of this world is painted vividly in the work of graphic artist and evangelist Jack T. Chick. Chick is one of the most controversial and widely read comic writer/artists of all time.

With a print run of over half a billion self-published tracts that have been translated into over one hundred different languages, Chick's work has been smuggled over countless borders, dropped into isolated African villages, and left in bathrooms throughout the world.

Chick's comic tracts have a number of recurring themes. But the one that is virtually ubiquitous involves an individual who must choose whether or not to accept Jesus as Lord and Savior. At the end of the tract, depending upon the person's decision, she is either depicted as meeting God in heaven or burning in a fiery lake, often with demons mocking her if she has made the wrong decision.

One of the interesting features about these tracts is the depiction of God as one who dwells above and beyond us. Alongside this is the image of a forsaken world, a world which can never satisfy and which will soon pass away.

It is very clear in Chick tracts that God is presently out of reach and that the role of the Church is to prepare people for an encounter with this God in the next life. Once someone has accepted Christ, the tract generally skips to this final reconciliation. The message is thus loud and clear: Eternal life begins after this one. God is to come.

For Chick, the Good News of Christianity is that there will one day be a time when we encounter God and experience profound peace, joy, and happiness. Until that time we must try to help as many people as possible to make a decision that will ensure they, too, will experience this final reconciliation. The result is that the Good News is meant for a future time, that the

Eternal Life referred to in the Gospels relates to a mode of life that begins after this one.

While Chick's tracts depict this philosophy in an extreme way, they merely reflect what we find in most Churches today: God stands over and above the world, and while God may be glimpsed at work, we must wait for the next life before we can be truly satisfied.

Here the world becomes a theater of melancholy, for it cannot satisfy us in any meaningful way. It is something that we must ultimately endure. Perhaps we gain some pleasure in it from time to time, but nothing in comparison to what lies ahead and thus nothing that we should attach ourselves too strongly to. Here religious practices (such as prayer, worship, service to the poor, fasting, etc.) never fully satisfy the soul but rather express our dedication and help us to focus upon the next life. In this way the practices involve a type of world-renunciation in which we attempt to detach from this world in preparation for the next, perhaps gaining brief glimpses into what lies ahead.

IN CONTRAST TO THIS, there are people who claim God is at work in the world and that we can have a deep relationship with Him here and now that looks somewhat like the kind of relationship we might have with any other thing in the world. We do not have to wait to meet the absolute but rather can, through a variety of means, meet God in a real way right now. We see this perspective played out particularly clearly in the charismatic and Pentecostal world: God is here and can be encountered as such.

This is testified to in ecstatic experiences that are often achieved during prayer and worship sessions in which the congregation experiences profound joy.

However, much as the universe that Chick presents to us, this is also a world-renouncing approach to faith, for while there is an experience of God accessible to us here and now, it takes place under exceptional circumstances. A distinction is thus maintained between the natural, mundane world and the supernatural realm of pure unadulterated joy. Not only this, but people can become so obsessed with the experiences they receive in a religious context that they become addicted to the Sunday morning service, the next big worship event, or the upcoming prayer ministry session. True meaning, from this perspective, is found in the exceptional times that happen once a week, year, or lifetime, rather than in the very midst of our everyday world. Here religious practices such as prayer, worship, service to the poor, and fasting are seen as able to bring us into direct contact with God, leaving the other times in our life less meaningful and establishing a distinction between sacred and secular. In addition to this, there are numerous people who affirm the view that God can be encountered here and now, yet who experience nothing. It is always the person to their left or right who is feeling the power of the Spirit or hearing the divine voice. For these people, even the places where God is supposed to show up become sites of disappointment.

In both of these responses (where God is believed to await us in the next life or is something we can encounter here in specific places or states), life as a whole itself is negated, and we are left unable to fully embrace and enjoy it. In religious terms, God is an object who is either totally distant or only present at very specific, highly regulated times.

The Now in the Not Yet

In order to understand this, let us consider the Looney Tunes cartoons where Wile E. Coyote is in obsessive pursuit of his arch-nemesis, the Roadrunner. The question that we might ask while watching this cartoon is: What would happen if Wile E. Coyote ever actually caught him? We can imagine that he would be deeply satisfied for a few days, but then he would start to feel lost. What is he to do now that he's finally gotten what he always wanted?

The problem is that when we get what we are driven to achieve, we discover that it does not actually give us the eternal joy we thought it would. When we get what we long so much for, we discover, like Wile E. Coyote, that there is a day after the kill, and a day after that.

This would lead to a growing sense of anxiety that could eventually plunge him into despair.

Alternatively, Wile E. Coyote could renounce his pursuit of the Roadrunner. But in this situation, he would retain the dream of catching him and thus never really be happy with anything else. He would yearn for the chase and imagine, over and over, catching the elusive bird. Nothing else he ever pursued would match up to the goal he had given up.

Does this mean that the only solution for Wile E. Coyote is to keep up the pursuit, secretly sabotaging his own efforts (using defective equipment, old ropes, etc.), so that he never catches the Roadrunner? This would seem to be a depressing answer and one that would be hard to keep up for long.

So are these his only options? Getting what he wants and despairing, not getting what he wants and despairing, constantly chasing what he wants and despairing? And, of course, are these our only options: experiencing God and finding out that life really isn't that different in the aftermath, not getting God and feeling empty, constantly chasing God and never finding rest?

In contrast, we are introduced to a radically different way of understanding God's presence in the Resurrection. Here we no longer approach God as an object that we love. Indeed, the idea of loving God directly becomes problematic. Instead, we learn that God is present in the very act of love itself. We do not find happiness by renouncing the world and pointing our desire toward the divine, but now we discover the divine in our very act of loving the world. God is loved through the work of love itself (Matthew 18:20, 1 John 4:20). It is in love that we find new meaning, joy, and fulfillment.

This is why the idea of God being love is such good news. For when we love, we gain what we desire while remaining at a distance from it.

To use another analogy from the world of cartoons, love operates like the black circles in Roadrunner that act as portals into an unending void. The circle is small enough to fold up and put in our pocket, and yet, when it is placed on the ground, we can jump into it. In the same way, the flesh of our beloved is experienced as taking up so little space, and yet our beloved is the very site of an inner universe without end. The other whom we love is not a mystery revealed to us but a mystery we are privileged, so privileged, to touch. When one falls in love, the person to whom one's attentions are directed takes on a sublime significance. It is as if that one person stands out from all others, rising above the crowd, embodying all that is beautiful and perfect. Kierkegaard caught this feeling wonderfully when he wrote of his beloved, Regina.

> O, can I really believe the poets when they say that the first time one sees the beloved object he thinks he has seen her long before, that love like all knowledge is recollection, that love in the single individual also has its prophecies, its types, its myths, its Old Testament. Everywhere, in the face of every girl, I see features of your beauty, but I think I would have to possess the beauty of all the girls in the world to extract your beauty.[3]

In love, the other, who is a frail, broken human being like everyone else, is cherished not *despite* her failings but *in* them. We do not ignore the fact she is a mere mortal, but rather find, in her very humanity, something truly sacred. There is no additional something that shines out of her that we attach ourselves to; rather, our love enables us to "see" her in her totality as sublime.

When God is treated as an object that we love, then we always experience a distance between ourselves and the ultimate source of happiness and meaning. But when God is found in love itself, then the very act of loving brings us into immediate relationship with the deepest truth of all. In love, the fragile, broken, temporal individual or cause that draws forth our desire becomes the very site where we find pleasure and peace. God no longer pulls on us as something "out there"; rather, God is a presence that is made manifest in our very midst. Here meaning is not found in turning away from the world but in fully embracing it through the act of love.

While love cannot be directly seen, love in a very specific way enables us to see. For in daily life we perceive others in much the same way as a cow gazes at cars. We walk past thousands of people every week, not necessarily seeing any of them. I was reminded of this recently when a friend of mine told me of something that happened when she took a train from Connecticut to New York. As the conductor—a large and imposing man—approached, she realized that she had left her purse at the house. When he got to her seat and asked for her ticket, she, with much embarrassment, explained the situation and braced herself for the worst. But the conductor sat down in the seat opposite and said, "Don't worry about it." Then, for the remainder of the journey, they talked. They shared photos of their families, they exchanged jokes, and they spoke of the ones who meant most to them. When the conductor finally got up to continue his rounds, my friend began to apologize again, but the conductor stopped her midsentence and smiled. "Please don't pay it any thought; you know, it's just really nice to be seen by someone."

This might initially seem like a strange thing to say as the conductor was seen by thousands of people every day. But only in instrumental terms, only as the extension of a function he performed. In this brief conversation with my friend, he felt he had actually been seen as a unique individual, and that was a gift to him.

This is what love does. It does not make itself visible but, like light, makes others visible to us. In a very precise sense, then, love's presence cannot be described as existing, but rather is that which calls others into existence; for to exist literally means to stand forth from the background, *to be brought forth*. As we have mentioned, love does not stand forth and vie for our attention but rather brings others forth. When we love, our beloved is brought out of the vast, undulating sea of others. Just as the Torah speaks of God calling forth beings from the formless ferment of being, so love calls our beloved out from the endless ocean of undifferentiated objects.

In this way love is not proud and arrogant. It does not say, "I am sublime, I am beautiful, I am glorious." Love humbly points to others and whispers, "They are sublime, they are beautiful, they are glorious."

Love does seek out our hymns of praise and prayers of adoration. Love does not want our sacrifices or seek our time. For love always points toward another. To honor love is to be in love, to swim in the world illuminated by love.

Is this not the properly theological understanding of God? Not a being we directly love, but rather the depth present in the very act of love itself. Not as one who seeks to be glorified but as the cause of glorification itself?

Whether or not the world has some ultimate meaning, love births meaning, brings meaning into the world, and renders the world meaningful even amidst the feeling that everything is fleeting. In love, the world is transfigured and rendered wonderful. God, in Christianity, is revealed as the source and depth of this transformation of the mundane into the sublime.

Christianity has been called the religion of love not because Christians are more loving but because of the way that it transitions us from the idea that the highest truth is to be loved to the idea that the highest truth is love itself.

Where Is God in Christ?

Let us approach this idea of God as the source and depth of love itself by reflecting briefly upon what it means to claim that a man dying upon a cross is God. The Christian does not claim this individual is God because he has some superpowers or that this human has some additional physical appendage that makes him God. If we were to cut open the body of Jesus, we would not find two hearts or some unique cellular structure. One person sees a dying man; another sees the Son of God. But this difference cannot be accounted for by saying that one had better eyesight than the other or a better view of the Crucifixion.

It is only those who love Christ who see Christ as God, for God is only visible there in the love and devotion of the disciples. This is the theological expression of what we find in romantic love when the beloved is, in the act of love itself, seen as absolute.

In the Incarnation, then, we find a fundamental transformation in the way that we are to approach God, a shift that takes us away from the religious understanding, which treats God as an object worthy of love, to a religionless understanding in which God is found in the very act of love itself. Loving God in a direct way is thus closed off in Christianity. Instead, in the very act of loving, God is (indirectly) loved. In the very mode of seeing that raises the suffering, broken, and excluded to the level of the beautiful, sublime, and absolute, God is present. Not dwelling behind or above, but as dwelling in the very midst. The mystery of God is a mystery that is found in the very heart of life itself.

This is why religious experience cannot be properly approached as an experience at all. To experience is to encounter *something*. But in the Incarnation, Crucifixion, and Resurrection we discover that God is not something we encounter directly and thus is not some-*thing* that we experience. Rather, God is that which transforms how we experience everything, i.e., love. God is the name we give to the way of living in which we experience the world as worthy of living for, fighting for, and dying for.

Traditionally we are brought to love the world because we love God and God loves the world. But once we fully embrace the understanding of God testified to in Christ, the middle reference that stands between us and the world dissolves entirely; we no longer love the world because God loves it, but rather we simply love the world and, in doing so, express our love for God.

This is why we must, with Bonhoeffer, avoid thinking that God's transcendence has anything to do with being outside the world. About such things none of us have any insider information. Rather, in Christianity God is an immanent transcendence. In other words, in the Incarnation we find that the mystery of God is not above us, nor is it negated in the world, but rather God dwells as a mystery in the very midst, present in the very act of raising the world itself to the level of the sublime.

God Is the Not Yet Who Is Now

The religious approach to God drains life of its pleasure through offering an elusive being from beyond who one must either accept is never fully present (thus rendering our faith practices into ultimately tedious disciplines), whom we think we can have but never encounter (making us feel excluded and unworthy), or who appears to us in exceptional moments (thus causing us to pursue ever more extreme religious practices that might create a "thin space" for these meetings). To approach God as a person we will meet in a future time, a person who is always avoiding us or whom we occasionally bump into, like some friend at a party, misses the properly theological insight that God is manifest only in our embrace and affirmation of the broken world.

In this post-Crucifixion understanding of the divine, we can have fullness of life here and now. Not because we somehow transcend our suffering and doubt, but because we are now able to bear their weight. God is not approached as some being who shows up on the scene occasionally to give gold teeth and a parking space, but rather is approached as that mysterious Otherness discovered in the very affirmation of the other. *God is love.* And thus God is present where we love. This is good news, this is life everlasting. For when we directly forget about God and turn away our own self-interested desires for meaning, immortality, and purity, when lose ourselves in love for the other; then, and only then, do we (indirectly) find God. This is what Bonhoeffer described so beautifully when he said,

> And we cannot be honest unless we recognise that we have
> to live in the world *etsi deus non daretur* [even if there were no
> God]. And this is just what we do recognize—before God!
> God himself compels us to recognize it. So our coming of
> age leads us to a true recognition of our situation before God.
> God would have us know that we must live as men who
> manage our lives without him. The God who is with us is the
> God who forsakes us (Mark 15:34). The God who lets us live
> in the world without the working hypothesis of God is the
> God before whom we stand continually. Before God and with
> God we live without God. God lets himself be pushed out of
> the world on to the cross. He is weak and powerless in the
> world, and that is precisely the way, the only way, in which
> he is with us and helps us. Matt. 8:17 makes it quite clear

that Christ helps us, not by virtue of his omnipotence, but by virtue of his weakness and suffering.[4]

In this very act of forsaking the religious God, along with all the psychological comfort that comes with it, we can find a way of fully affirming God—not in some belief we affirm but in the material practice of love. So then, as we turn away from the obsessive desire to find fulfillment, meaning, and acceptance, we come into direct contact with them. This is life before death; this is life in all its fullness.

Do You Believe in God?

What we discover here is that the question, *Does God exist?* is not a straightforward one for the believer. Within the contemporary debate concerning the existence of God, the issue seems unambiguous, and everyone agrees with what the question means. But the believer needs to ask a more fundamental question than this. That is: What does it mean to claim that God exists?

In much of the popular debate, the meaning of the word "existence" is taken by all sides to describe some *thing*, an object that can be reflected upon by an external observer. But this notion of existence is one that the believer ought to reject when approaching the question of God. In such debates the argument revolves around whether there is some supreme being that brought everything that is into existence. In response to this one can answer with *Yes* (theism of some variety), *No* (empirical atheism), *I don't know* (weak agnosticism), *no one can know* (strong agnosticism), or *the question is irrelevant* (ignosticism).

However, from a Christological perspective, the question itself, which everyone seems to take for granted, now comes to signify something else entirely. Instead of the words, *Do you believe in God?* meaning *Do you believe there is empirical data to assent to the existence of an extra-linguistic Supreme Being governing the universe?*, it now refers to a way in which one lives and breathes. The empirical rendering of the question may continue to interest the philosopher and it is no doubt a fascinating conversation to have with friends over a drink. But it is not a specifically theological question when taken in this way. For the believer who passes through the Christian experience, God is no longer related to as an object *out there*. Rather, God is affirmed only through a passionate participation in life itself.

This means that we can no longer claim that we know God while hating our neighbor. Those who have taken part in the event of Conversion (participation in Crucifixion and Resurrection) cannot claim to believe in God except insofar as love emanates from them, transforming the world within which they are embedded.

In other words, the claim *I believe in God* is nothing but a lie if it is not manifest in our lives, because one only believes in God insofar as one loves.

In the Resurrection faith testified to in the New Testament, the question *Do you believe in God?* is transformed and now involves the very being of the one asking the question. As such it can be rendered in this way: *Is your entire being caught up in a commitment to embracing the world?* In Christianity, to believe in God means nothing other than to be the site where love is born, where to find the courage to affirm the world and live fully into it.

So for the Christian, a new range of answers to the question *Do you believe in God?* arises. Answers such as, *I aspire to, ask my friends,* or more importantly, *talk to my enemies.*

Of course, the idea that belief in God is manifested in nothing other than the Christ-like tenure of our existence will strike much of the actually existing church as heresy. It suggests that one cannot claim to have knowledge of God if one does not exhibit a life of boundless love. Yet isn't this the type of heresy that brings us close to the very heart of orthodox Christianity? As the book of James makes clear, the demons of hell can be said to have the correct empirical understanding of reality, and yet it does them no good at all.

O Death, Where Is Thy Sting?

To approach what Resurrection life might feel like, let's consider the myth of Sisyphus. In this ancient story, King Sisyphus is punished by the gods with the curse of having to spend eternity carrying out an utterly meaningless task—he is forced to push a large boulder to the top of a steep hill, only to watch it roll back to the bottom, whereupon he must once more push it to the top. Philosopher Albert Camus once famously employed this myth as a metaphor for human life. He argued that we tend to imagine that what we do has some kind of external significance, though really we are engaged in an endless round of pointless tasks with no purpose.

The theological response here is that it makes no difference whether or not we believe this vision to be true, nor whether or not this vision is true. Rather, in the experience of Crucifixion, we existentially confront the psychological power of this vision. It is in our participation in the Crucifixion that we feel it to be true.

In the Crucifixion we lose the idea of God as the one who justifies our loving engagement with the world by approving of it, but in Resurrection we continue to affirm God as we love the world regardless. This is the move that some of the Christian mystics spoke of, a move from the idolatry of doing good for some reason (to get to heaven, please God, get approval from others), to the act of doing good for no external reward. The former can be described as works-based, in that it involves an economic exchange. I do something in order to get a (divine) return. In the latter, we lay down all desire for reward and, in doing so, experience how love is its own reward. In the very experience of being forsaken by God (Crucifixion) we find God in the very affirmation of life itself (Resurrection).

In short, we come into contact with the truth of Incarnation.

IN THIS NEW WAY of being, one does not say "yes" to existence because of some external source but because existence is experienced as wondrous in itself. Here we find that we are able to affirm life, even in the very midst of unknowing and uncertainty.

In this new state, the world is affirmed in the deepest and most radical way, not because everything that happens in it is good (indeed, all too often the very opposite is true), but because, in love, we experience creation, in all its brokenness, as wonderful. This idea is expressed powerfully in a reflection offered by Nietzsche in what is known as the myth of eternal return. In *The Gay Science* he writes,

> What if some day or night a demon were to steal after you into your loneliest loneliness and say to you: "This life as you now live it and have lived it, you will have to live once more and innumerable times more" . . . Would you not throw yourself down and gnash your teeth and curse the demon who spoke thus? Or have you once experienced a tremendous moment when you would have answered him: "You are a god and never have I heard anything more divine."[5]

In this reflection Nietzsche contrasts two different responses one can have to the revelation that one's life would repeat again and again exactly as it has played out thus far. One response to such an idea would be to fall into the pit of utter despair, cursing the gods for such a horrific torture, while the other would involve the much more difficult act of embracing the eternal recurrence with joy.

By making a demon the harbinger of this message, Nietzsche is making it clear that such an idea initially sounds diabolical, something that Nietzsche would have acutely felt due to prolonged illness and a failed love affair that scarred his life. As such, Nietzsche had no intention of making this some moral tale about the beauty of existence. Abuse, rape, torture, and illness are horrific realities that he was well aware of. Rather, Nietzsche is asking whether one can truly affirm life as such, even in the very midst of all the suffering and pain. If we are able to say "yes" to life when confronted with the possibility of repeating everything, then such a demonic curse is robbed of its sting.

Take the example of free association in psychoanalysis. In contrast to the popular idea that analysis begins with the act of free association (where a person speaks out what is on their mind in a free-flowing way), it can be said that the ability to free-associate signals that the patient is approaching the end of therapy. In other words, people are often unable to free-associate when they first go to analysis because there are so many traumas that they cannot return to. Their inability to speak of their pain testifies to its power and destruction. But when a patient can bring to mind and freely talk about difficult parts of their life without pain, this can signal that they have been able to rob them of their power. In other words, it is only as we learn how to return to them without experiencing their initial horror that we are able to simultaneously move beyond them.

Resurrection faith is then manifested in a freedom and liberation in which we are able to courageously and fully embrace this world without repression, resentment, and fear. It is a way of living in love, a love that embraces existence, not because it is perfect, but because it is beautiful in the midst of its very imperfection.

This does not mean that we stop experiencing anxiety and sadness—not at all—but that in the very midst of these we still find life worth living. We no longer need to hide from our sadness and repress it. Rather, we can confront it and work through it. Indeed, it is the very acceptance of our sadness that can lead to its dissipation. Just as grace (the experience of accepting that we are accepted as we are) enables us to change, so too, by accepting that we must mourn (rather than run from it) we can ourselves move through our pain (rather than having it return again and again in various masked forms).

Here, death is robbed of its sting (1 Corinthians 15:55) and despair is overcome. This is indeed the testimony of the early Church regarding Jesus of Nazareth; in the earliest Christian writings on the Incarnation, we read of people who witnessed an individual fully immersed in the human condition (Jesus, the human being) and yet who existed in a state of continual overcoming (Christ, the divine life).

All this means that the event of Resurrection opens up a type of *religionless* faith in which we are able to embrace the world and ourselves without some security blanket. It is here, amidst the ashes of the death of the deus ex machina, that a different understanding of God becomes visible. This God is affirmed where people are gathered together in love and is testified to where the sick are healed, the starving fed, and where those who dwell in death are raised into life. "Where two or three come together in my name," we read in the Gospel according to Matthew, "there am I with them."[6] In other words, where people are gathered together in love, God is present.

We Are Destiny

This deeply Christological approach fundamentally critiques the pagan idea that there is some overarching Destiny within which the seeming chaos of life finds its purpose. From this perspective there is cosmic blueprint held in some celestial abode. Everything that happens does so for a reason, and we must come to accept our place in the grand scheme.

This does not mean, however, that we ought to reject the idea of destiny. For in Christ, we come into contact with another possibility, one that is expressed beautifully in the parable that opens this chapter. For what if Resurrection life is marked by the acceptance of our role as *creators* of destiny rather than mere pawns to be moved around by it? In the Christological frame, the idea of destiny remains, but it is understood as forged through the free acts of those dedicated to the bringing of life. Here destiny no longer refers to some predetermined reality that history conforms to, but rather comes into being through our direct participation in the transformation of the world. In short, *we participate in the creation of the eternal itself.*

This approach is deeply theological in nature; however, one can find an interesting analogy from the world of science. In modern physics, there is a famous thought experiment called Schrödinger's cat (in honor of the physicist Erwin Schrödinger, who devised it). Originally it was conceived as an attempt to draw out the logical absurdity of what is called the Copenhagen interpretation of quantum mechanics. In the quantum world it was discovered that particles manifest themselves in different ways depending upon how they are observed—light, for example, will act as either a wave or a particle depending on how it is measured. The Copenhagen interpretation of this phenomenon claims that a particle remains in what is called a superposition until it is measured in some way. Only then does it "collapse" into a definite state.

In order to try to show how incoherent this idea was, Schrödinger imagined a device within which one would place a cat. Inside the device there would be a minuscule piece of radioactive material and a Geiger counter. The radioactive material would be of such a size that, within an hour, it was possible for one of the atoms to decay. He imagined that the device would be set up so that, if an atom did decay, gas would be released into the device and the cat would die. In this way there were two possibilities, either an atom would decay and the cat would die, or none would decay and the cat would live.

According to Schrödinger, the Copenhagen interpretation would imply that the atoms are suspended in a superposition until someone actually looked at the Geiger counter. Here Schrödinger claimed that this would mean that the cat would effectively be both alive and dead until someone looked, at which point the atoms would collapse into a particular state, and the cat would either be dead or alive. More than this, the cat would always have been in whatever state it was observed in (either alive or dead). In short, until observed, the cat was both alive and dead, and it only took one of those states through the involvement of an observer. The very act of looking at the cat in the present would then bring into being the past. While there are some problems with the thought experiment (for example, the Geiger counter itself measures what the atom is doing and so will affect the state of the atoms), it actually describes something profoundly accurate concerning how the quantum world seems to function. While Schrödinger wanted to use the thought experiment to draw out an absurdity, the reality is that at present, the Copenhagen interpretation is a valid one. This means that measurement in the present may well cause something to take a particular form. *Here the act of participation creates the reality that one participates in.*

In theological terms, one can say that destiny exists in a type of superposition that only collapses into a particular form through the courageous, free act of believers working together for the good of the world. The properly Christian answer to the question of what God's will is for my life is thus:

Everything that has brought me to this very moment, the moment in which I must resolutely decide the next step without any cosmic support.

Because destiny is open, freedom and responsibility are thrust upon us. There is no plan B, no army of angels ready to descend into the world if we fail to reach out to our neighbor. In Resurrection life we find the courage to face up to this terrifying freedom, we grow the muscles needed to bear its weight, and we discover the compassion required to act. In this new mode of life, we find the conviction required to fully assume responsibility for our fleeting, fragile existence. We are unchained from the shackles that would bind us to some divine script already written and instead experience destiny as something we participate in through a full and loving embrace of the world.

Chapter Seven

I Believe in the Insurrection

Just as it was written by those prophets of old, the last days of the
Earth overflowed with suffering and pain. In those dark days a huge
pale horse rode through the Earth with Death upon its back and Hell
in its wake. During this great tribulation, the Earth was scorched with
the fires of war, rivers ran red with blood, the soil withheld its fruit,
and disease descended like a mist. One by one, all the nations of the
Earth were brought to their knees.

Far from all the suffering, high up in the heavenly realm, God
watched the events unfold with a heavy heart. An ominous silence
had descended upon Heaven as the angels witnessed the Earth
being plunged into darkness and despair. But as this could only
continue for so long, at the designated time, God stood upright,
breathed deeply, and addressed the angels, "The time has now come
for me to separate the sheep from the goats, the healthy wheat from
the inedible chaff."

Having spoken these words, God slowly turned to face the world *and called forth to the Church with a booming voice, "Rise up and ascend to Heaven, all of you who have who have sought to escape the horrors of this world by sheltering beneath my wing. Come to me, all who have turned from this suffering world by calling out, 'Lord, Lord.'"*

In an instant millions where caught up in the clouds and ascended into the heavenly realm, leaving the suffering world behind them.

Once this great rapture had taken place, God paused for a moment and then addressed the angels, saying, "It is done. I have separated the people born of my spirit from those who have turned from me. It is time now for us leave this place and take up residence on the Earth, for it is there that we shall find our people: the ones who would forsake Heaven in order to embrace the Earth, the few who would turn away from eternity itself to serve at the feet of a fragile, broken life that passes from existence in but an instant."

And so it was that God and the heavenly host left that place to dwell among those who had rooted themselves upon the Earth: the ones who had forsaken God for the world and thus who bore the mark of God; the few who had discovered Heaven in the very act of forsaking it.

The Violence of Resurrection

So far we have introduced the Resurrection as a mode of living that embraces the lived experience of doubt, complexity, and unknowing, affirms life, and accepts our responsibility in transforming the world. In this way Resurrection houses a deep violence, an ethical violence. This is not a violence directed against individuals, but rather a violence against those systems that would oppress, destroy, and bring death. People like Martin Luther King, Jr., in his pacifism express this Christian violence beautifully, for in his nonparticipation in institutionalized racism and uncompromising stance against passive involvement with oppressive norms, he directly expressed an alternative vision of the world. In his seductive picture of a new world and unrelenting quest to see its realization in reality, he ruptured the corrupt systems of power that surrounded him. In this way he expressed the violence expressed by Paul in Ephesians,

> For our struggle is not against flesh and blood, but against the rulers, against the authorities, against the powers of this dark world and against the spiritual forces of evil in the heavenly realms.[1]

Paul is not shying away from the fact that Resurrection life plants us into the very heart of a battle. But this is not a battle against people; rather it is one that sets itself against systems that oppress people, preventing their development into fully responsible, ethical individuals. It is this direct attack against prevailing structures, such as ineffective school systems or unjust legal structures, that can facilitate real change in society.

This is why we may say that the type of violence we witness in fundamentalism is actually a form of impotence similar to that of a man who beats his wife. The horrific acts are testimony to his own weakness, his inability to face up to the true situation and change it.

For all the militant talk that we find in fundamentalist communities, it is easy to perceive a basic desire to maintain structures of oppression and the status quo. Their often sexist, homophobic, and racist rhetoric is aimed firmly at maintaining their position of power and thus is designed specifically to prevent change. Their violence is the horrific manifestation of their desire to keep things as they are.

In contrast, a true Christian militant attacks systems of oppression and fights for a better world, even though that new world might negatively affect their own position of power. It is then a violence that cuts against the very one who joins the fight. Christian violence is the public expression of love; it is that work which ruptures systems of abuse, robbing them of their power and efficiency. It is manifest in the formation of insurrectionary groups that live out a radically different mode of social relation, one that challenges the system by offering an alternative vision of the world. If our lives simply contribute to maintaining the status quo and if our faith does not challenge injustice at a fundamental level (instead focusing on subjective feelings and matters of personal piety), then we are not engaged in the battle Paul describes.

When Trying to Change the System Ensures That It Never Changes

One of the ways that we avoid taking on the idea that we are destiny and throwing ourselves into the Pauline battlefield is through the embrace of token gestures—some small act that, while perhaps doing some immediate good, masks how the rest of one's life runs counter to it and undermines it. Token gestures enable us to support a positive self-image, helping to maintain the plausibility of the story we tell ourselves about ourselves.

The logic of the token gesture can be seen played out in the *Batman* films. Here Bruce Wayne is presented as having an obsession with stamping out street violence, an obsession that arises as a direct result of witnessing his mother and father brutally murdered by a thief on the streets of Gotham.

The initial question we are faced with concerns whether his crime-fighting antics at the weekend really serve to make any real difference in Gotham. There is, after all, only one Batman for the whole city. As one criminal remarks in *The Dark Knight,* you would have more chance of winning the lottery than bumping into him. This question is directly addressed in *The Dark Knight;* however, there is a much more fundamental issue that remains unexplored. In order for Bruce Wayne to fund his high-tech, covert military campaign against the criminals of Gotham, he must secretly siphon off vast sums of money from Wayne Industries, the business that he owns. The amount he pours into his work would run into the millions, if not billions.

When confronted by this, one must wonder whether it might not be much more effective if he took that money and spent it on developing a strong educational system within the city, setting up training programs for the unemployed, and helping small businesses develop.

Of course, the Joker, his main adversary, has little interest in money (burning vast sums in front of the Mafia to prove his point), and there will always be some who simply live to create chaos. However, a city without the infrastructure to provide good education and work opportunities simply feeds the Joker's evil schemes by sustaining the conditions that lead to a large underclass unable to find representation in the city. Batman's archvillains would have a difficult time carrying out their crimes if they did not have an unlimited number of poor and desperate people to prey upon, people who turn to crime in order to survive and find identity. If Batman spent his time and money supporting a life-giving infrastructure, the crime wave in Gotham might be broken.

The problem, however, lies in the fact that Bruce Wayne is too invested in his crime-fighting antics. For he often seems to get his meaning from actually engaging in a direct way with crime, doing what he does not because he is interested in transforming Gotham City, but because he wants to feel the pleasure of taking revenge. If this is indeed the case, then Bruce Wayne needs the criminals in order to experience the cathartic release of directly attacking them.

Do we not often experience something similar in our charitable giving?

To give to someone in need can make us feel good. We can even gain much more than we give in these situations. But what if our real job is not to give to those who are poor but to help create a world where the poor do not exist?

What if the Church should be less concerned with creating saints than creating a world where we do not need saints? A world where people like Mother Teresa and MLK would have nothing to do.

This leads us to another question: What if Bruce Wayne would not really want to dedicate his life to real structural change because it might negatively affect his position in society? For if he really did change the city through creating better education and more opportunities for work, might this not create an environment where monopolies like Wayne Industries would be challenged? By really changing things, Bruce Wayne might actually create a world where his own lifestyle is challenged.

By avoiding these questions, Bruce Wayne is able to look and feel like he is part of the solution when, in his overall material practices, he is really a part of the problem. It is one thing to beat up a criminal; it's another to commit oneself to the difficult task of transforming society. Thus, while Bruce Wayne wears a mask to protect his crime fighting identity from others, the very Batman persona is itself a mask that shields Bruce Wayne from confronting his own true identity.

We can see a real-life example of this in the life of eighteenth-century theologian Jonathan Edwards. Edwards was a slave owner who strongly advocated the fair treatment of slaves, condemning the policy of taking people from Africa. However, he never directly attacked the system that sustained slavery. This move was left to people like his son, who questioned the very conditions that supported slavery. The point was not to be kind to one's slaves but to create a world where slavery did not exist.

What we begin to learn here is the way that the very act of

trying to change the system can be an important part of ensuring that the system never changes. The affirmation of oppressive structures, relationships, or employment and the attempt to change them through token gestures are simply two sides of the same coin—or two sides of a Möbius strip.

When Attacking the System Ensures That It Never Changes

We have seen how token gestures aimed at changing a system are actually a vital part of how that system supports itself. However, there is another, perhaps more surprising reality, than this. For often our direct and passionate protests against a system are themselves part of what that system needs in order to run effectively. This type of protest can be called a perverse protest, for a perverse structure is one that upholds and draws out the power of that which it appears to resist.

In order to understand how perverse protests work, let us take the example of a person saying, "This time next year, I am going to leave this dead-end job and travel the world." While the person might sincerely mean this, we also know that most people who say this are unlikely to act on it. We may wish to attribute this failure to act to a mere lack of conviction—and for certain people this might be the case—however, we also need to appreciate how this statement can function as a means of ensuring its failure. For often the idea of leaving a job functions as the very thing people need to hold onto in order to remain within the work. It is the lie that enables them to cope with the truth of their unhappiness.

This is something we see played out clearly in Michael Mann's film *Collateral*. Early on, we find out that the taxi driver Max (Jamie Foxx) has plans to set up a company called "Island Limousines," which would provide wealthy customers with the best service. He is so caught up in the pleasure this dream affords him that he even lies to his elderly mother, telling her that he already has the company. While initially we are led to believe that he really is making efforts to set up this company, as the film progresses, we begin to see that this desire is actually a pipe dream that enables him to function in the job that he hates. So long as he has this dream of something better just around the corner, he is able to put up with a bad boss, long hours, and bad pay. It takes the assassin riding in his taxi (Vincent) to act in the role of the analyst and point this out,

> Vincent: Look in the mirror . . . with your paper
> towels . . . clean cab . . . a limo company . . . someday.
> How much you got saved?
>
> Max: That ain't none of your business.
>
> Vincent: Someday, someday my dream will come?
> One night you'll wake up and you'll discover it never
> happened. It's all turned around on you, and it never
> will. Suddenly you are old. It didn't happen, and it never

will because you were never going to do it anyway. You'll push it into memory, then zone out in your Barcalounger, being hypnotized by daytime TV for the rest of your life. Don't you talk to me about murder. All it ever took was a down payment on a Lincoln Town Car, and that girl . . . you can't even call that girl. What are you still doing driving a cab?

This dialogue can help to expose what is meant by the literary term "suspension of disbelief." Suspension of disbelief basically describes the process in which we refuse to know what we know. This suspension is necessary if we are going to immerse ourselves in a story. For instance, while watching a film, we know full well that we are looking at a screen and that what we are watching are actors engaged in a fiction constructed by writers, directors, producers, etc. However, we suspend this knowledge so as to enter into and enjoy what we are watching. We both know and don't know at one and the same time. This means that we are able to watch a horror film and be truly scared without screaming and calling the police.

This suspension of disbelief does not, however, limit itself to our engagement with books and films. For example, a teenager might engage in this act when he goes to speak with a college counselor. In order to speak freely about the issue that is on his mind, he may need to believe that the counselor really cares about him and sees him in a singular way. Yet the teenager is also aware that the counselor is there because she is being paid and that she is seeing hundreds of people like himself, people she likely cares little about. Or take the example of prostitution; often a man will need to believe that the woman is enjoying having sex in order to engage in the act. Yet the very exchange of money demonstrates that this is an exchange rather than something meaningful to the woman.

This structure of perverse protest is expressed in the *Matrix* trilogy. The films are set in the near future in the aftermath of a war between humans and self-conscious machines—a war the machines had won. The outcome was that humans were now used as an energy source, like batteries. While the physical body of a person is drained of its energy, the person's mind is plugged into software that generates a false world based upon the Earth as it was at the end of the twentieth century. In the first film, we learn that not all humans are enslaved and that there is in fact an active group of freedom fighters dedicated to destroying the machines. More than this, there is a hidden city where thousands of humans live in freedom and a Messianic figure who is believed by some to have the power to lead humans out of their slavery.

At the time of the first film, many Christians found helpful parallels between their own faith and the film. Neo, the trilogy's Messiah, came to represent Christ; the freedom fighters were viewed as Christians; and Zion symbolized the Church. More than this, the Matrix itself (the software that humans were plugged into) was used as an analogy for the sinful world that people need to be liberated from by the Gospel.

There was however a certain irony in this eager appropriation of the first film, for in the second and third installments, we discover something truly surprising. This group of freedom fighters who have dedicated themselves to the destruction of the machines are actually *supported by the machines*. The machines secretly encourage the freedom fighters, help them build Zion, and provide them with their Messiah. We learn that there have been many cities before Zion and many Messiahs before Neo. We thus discover that Neo is not really on the side of freedom but actually a vital part of the oppressive system itself. It turns out that the machines initially attempted to build a Matrix where rebellion was impossible, a world that was, however, modeled upon human perfection. But the results were disastrous; it failed. The machines realized that people needed to have the ability to fight. Hence they created release valves in the system, opportunities for people to resist in a way that was ultimately authorized by those in control. In short, the freedom fighters were the very thing that the system allowed in order to ensure nothing significant really changed. Indeed, true change only happens when an anomaly enters the world of the machines.

Perhaps those Church leaders who adopted the first film to their own ends were more right than they realized or would like to admit. By providing a system of insipid worship services and prayer meetings, they form spaces that enable people to think that they are part of a resistance group (talking about it and singing about it) while simultaneously feeding the system they say they oppose. These pseudotransgressions enable people to attack a structure in ways that are actually sanctioned by the structure. We get to feel like rebels (painting an image of ourselves as outcasts) while actually being nothing other than

supporters of the system (benefiting from all the spoils of supporting the systems of oppression).

Consider the way protest is managed under a government such
as China's. Protest is allowed only if the group fills in various pieces
of official paperwork, meet at a certain time in a certain designated
place, and disband at a predetermined point. In short, you are allowed to protest as long as the protest itself is managed in such a
way as to ensure it is not disruptive and has no potency. By creating a small amount of leniency within the law (allowing officially
sanctioned protests), the government appears to welcome possible
challenge. In this way the system masks its oppressive nature.

So we must be wary of how our community activities function.
Are we making a true difference or just participating in an ironic
act, throwing pebbles at the very system that we build with our
everyday actions?

When we are brought to the point of seeing this structure in our
own lives, we can experience the feeling of nihilism, something we witness in *Collateral* when Max realizes the perverse nature of his dream.

> But you know what? It doesn't matter. What's it matter,
> anyway? 'Cause we are . . . insignificant out here in this big-
> ass nowhere. Twilight Zone shit. Says the badass sociopath in
> my backseat. So that's one thing I got to thank you for, bro . . .
> Until now, I never saw it that way . . .

This dark moment is not unlike what we witness in Alcoholics
Anonymous when an individual admits to his problem. While it

is a traumatic and scary admission, it comes at the point when he has nothing left to lose and so much to gain. It is then a nihilistic space, but one that opens up the possibility of stepping into a new and vibrant reality.

Changing the System by Ignoring It

In contrast to token gestures and perverse protests, there is a different way: the way of Resurrection life. This is a way of living that is able to short-circuit the present social, spiritual, or political order, something that we witness at a political level in the life of Mother Teresa, who no more protested against the caste system in Calcutta than she affirmed it. She simply lived in a different reality. She lived as though it did not exist, helping all who came to her regardless of their social class. This act of living the not-yet state of equality as if it already existed in the now is the truly political act, an act that directly confronts unjust systems by ignoring them and living into a different reality.

The theorist Hakim Bey described this exercise of living an alternative reality in the midst of the present one as the creation of a Pirate Island. Pirate Islands were originally geographical communities that existed within the legal net of the British Empire, but which lived out a different set of values. They were small communities located within the dominant one and yet not defined by it. However, as the maps were completed, Pirate Islands became, for Bey, social spaces that existed in the Empire rather than just beyond it. In the same way, the ministries set up by Mother Teresa exist within a system and yet are distinct from it, paying no regard to the sectarian values that exist all around them.[2]

The difficult political question we must ask is: Do the activities we participate in as a church act as token gestures or perverse protests that end up supporting the system they supposedly oppose? Could our prayer meetings and weekly involvement with social justice programs actually operate as a means of preventing us from changing how we spend our time and energy the rest of the week, enabling us to continue in careers that contribute to the very things that we are praying against and acting in ways that contradict what we express in our Bible studies?

Is it not all too possible for us to continue to work tirelessly in a job with questionable ethical practices because we attend church once a week and volunteer at the local homeless shelter on a Thursday evening? These activities thus are impotent acts that simply alleviate the guilt that would otherwise make it difficult for us to embrace our true (social) self—the self expressed in what we do the rest of the week. Such supposedly ethical acts come to resemble the exercise of rearranging deck chairs on the *Titanic*—doing something that belies the fact that we are really doing nothing of any substance.

The point is that the story that we tell ourselves about ourselves combined with the superficial actions that help us to maintain this story (token gestures and perverse protest) together act as a veil that hides the reality of our negative or negligible impact in the world. The small acts that convince us we are living in a countercultural way (such as attending a prayer meeting once a week or volunteering for a local fundraiser) become the very things that prevent us from embracing the countercultural radical change that Resurrection signals.

Donating money to the poor without asking why the poor exist in the first place, for instance, allows us to alleviate our guilt without fundamentally challenging the system that perpetuates poverty. As the Brazilian archbishop Dom Helder Camara once said, "When I give food to the poor, they call me a saint. When I ask why the poor have no food, they call me a Communist."[3]

As the example of *Collateral* shows, this is related not only to wider political issues, but also our own more private life. For we must also ask whether engaging in various religious activities actually enables us to ignore the dysfunctional relationship we are in, the job we detest, or the illness that is making its mark on our life.

Pie in the Sky When You Die

In order to understand the difference between providing ways of supporting an oppressive system and of challenging it consider the difference between Joseph Webster's hymn "The Sweet By and By" and songwriter Joe Hill's famous parody of it. "The Sweet By and By" was originally inspired by a comment made by Webster (who composed the music) to S. Fillmore Bennett in 1868. It was well known that Webster was a sensitive man who was prone to bouts of depression. Bennett writes that Webster had come to his place of business in a melancholy mood one day. When asked what the matter was, Webster responded by saying,

"It's no matter, it will be all right by and by." Immediately Bennett was inspired and penned the words to the hymn. There and then Webster created a melody, and within thirty minutes they were singing it together. The famous refrain from the hymn is,

> *In the sweet by and by*
> *We shall meet on that beautiful shore;*
> *In the sweet by and by*
> *We shall meet on that beautiful shore.*

For Webster this song provided some psychological comfort by helping him live with his current problems by enabling him to imagine a heavenly realm where everything would be better. In this way he was able to console himself in this life with thoughts of another.

It was left to the labor activist and songwriter Joe Hill to expose the problem with this hymn in his parody entitled "The Preacher and the Slave," written in 1911. He composed this song in response to the fact that migrant workers would often be greeted by the Salvation Army singing "The Sweet By and By" as they returned to the city each evening after having worked all day in dire conditions. The hymn communicated to them that their life would begin after death and consoled them with the notion that one day, in the sweet by and by, they would be happy and content. The song had a certain power because it did *reflect* the people's suffering, and it was a *response* to it, but it was a response that prevented action that could concretely *address* the suffering.

In "The Preacher and the Slave," Hill parodied the idea that we just needed to wait for another life after this one (this song is where the phrase "pie in the sky when you die" originated). For Hill, life was possible before death, but only as we put our shoulder to the plow of historical struggle and fight for equality here and now. And so he wrote:

> *Long-haired preachers come out every night,*
> *Try to tell you what's wrong and what's right;*
> *But when asked how 'bout something to eat*
> *They will answer in voices so sweet*

> *Chorus (sung as a call and response)*

> *You will eat [You will eat] bye and bye [bye and bye]*
> *In that glorious land above the sky [Way up high]*
> *Work and pray [Work and pray] live on hay [live on hay]*
> *You'll get pie in the sky when you die [That's a lie!]*

> *And the Starvation Army, they play,*
> *And they sing and they clap and they pray,*
> *Till they get all your coin on the drum,*
> *Then they tell you when you're on the bum*

> *(Chorus)*

> *Holy Rollers and Jumpers come out*

And they holler, they jump and they shout
Give your money to Jesus, they say,
He will cure all diseases today

(Chorus)

If you fight hard for children and wife—
Try to get something good in this life—
You're a sinner and bad man, they tell,
When you die you will sure go to hell.

(Chorus)

Workingmen of all countries, unite
Side by side we for freedom will fight
When the world and its wealth we have gained
To the grafters we'll sing this refrain

Chorus (modified)

You will eat [You will eat] bye and bye [bye and bye]
When you've learned how to cook and how to fry [How to
fry]
Chop some wood [Chop some wood], 'twill do you good
[do you good]
Then you'll eat in the sweet bye and bye [That's no lie]

While this was not intended as a church hymn, does it not capture the spirit of what it might mean to embrace the life of Christ? This is something that was captured with the ripping of the temple veil at the Crucifixion, for there we are brought to the realization that faith is lived in this world. What existed on the other side of the veil was not God (as traditional theology asserts) but the priest. The hidden truth of Judaism is fully revealed in Christianity for all to see with the tearing of the veil: *Faith is about this life.* Here a new epoch is signaled, the epoch of the Holy Spirit. Here we learn that faith is lived out in love of the world. A love that does not satisfy itself in token gestures and perverse protests but which hungers for real, substantial transformation.

In this way Christianity can be described as a theological materialism: It is that which transforms our material existence. If our faith does not throw us into the arms of the world, if it does not lead to our experience of responsibility, love, celebration, and our commitment to transformation, then, whatever we call it, we have nothing but an empty shell.

The Call within a Call

The movement that we have been exploring thus far charts the development from the act of giving up everything for God (Jesus in the Garden of Gethsemane), through the act of giving up everything including God (Christ on the Cross) to the point at which we become the very site of God (Resurrection life). Each step on this journey is fraught with difficulties but also has its rewards. The person who does not even begin this journey will never know what it is like to risk everything for a cause. The individual who stays at the level of the religious sacrifice will find community and solidarity but will become caught up in the web of fundamentalism, while those who make it beyond this place, but who stay at the cross, will taste freedom but with it the onslaught of despair. It is as we move beyond that place of despair and find meaning in the very midst of this life, rather than beyond it, that we touch upon the truth testified to in the Gospels.

In order to understand this journey let us return once more to Mother Teresa. Her call to become a nun can be viewed as a concrete example of the religious sacrifice as it was the point when she gave up everything for God. It was some years later, however, when she experienced what she described as her "call within the call." This can be seen as nothing less than her identification with Christ on the Cross: here she loses everything, including God. This loss was not a fleeting experience that arose at small and insignificant intervals during her work but remained with her until the end. Something we glimpse in some retreat notes written by Mother Teresa in 1959 (ten years after her sense of being forsaken by God). Here she notes, "There was a burning zeal in my soul for souls from childhood until I said 'yes' to God and then all is gone. Now I don't believe."[4]

What we witness very directly in this movement from her original "call" to the "call within the call" is an embodiment of the radical message of the Gospels. In the call she stands with Christ in the Garden of Gethsemane (willing to lose everything *for* God) while in the call within the call she hangs with Christ on the Cross (losing everything *including* God). This is the transition from the ultimate religious sacrifice to the sacrifice of religion itself. The latter event does not supersede the former but rather deepens it. Mother Teresa beautifully articulates this idea in the way that she describes the second event, not in terms of some separate or higher call, but rather as a call that takes place within the original call, a call that redoubles itself. A call that fulfills the initial one by delving ever more deeply into its unfathomable depths.

For Mother Teresa there was in all of this a deep inner agony and emptiness. For instance she writes, "No faith, no love, not even feeling . . . the darkness is so dark, and the pain so painful." And also, "I have nothing—since I have not Him—whom my heart and soul longs to possess. Aloneness is so great—From within and from without I find no one to turn to . . . If there is hell—then this must be one . . . no prayer, no faith, no love." And yet those who knew her most intimately testify to a deep joy and biting humor, of a soul full of passion and life. So how are we to reconcile this seeming paradox?

It is well known that Mother Teresa attempted to have the correspondence between herself and her spiritual advisors destroyed, repeatedly asking those who had letters regarding her private motivations to ensure that they never became public. Initially one might think that her reason for seeking the destruction of this correspondence was related to some kind of dark private sin that she wanted to hide. However, the letters are beautiful expressions of a woman with singular integrity and passion, a woman who wrestled with a sense of divine absence while devoting her life to the way of Jesus.

In light of her concern that her correspondence would be made public, many have claimed that it was her experience of divine absence that she was afraid of revealing. Yet this does not get to the heart of Mother Teresa's attempts to have the letters destroyed. What we find instead is that she is primarily concerned that people's interest in her subjective experience might take away from what is truly important: the work itself. For instance we read,

> From Monsignor E. Barber I heard that Cardinal Spellman wants to write about me and the work. Bishop Morrow is going to come to ask you for all the documents. With you and Fr. Van Exem I have entrusted my deepest thoughts—my love for Jesus—and His tender love for me—please do not give anything of 1946. I want the work to remain only His. When the beginning will be known, people will think more of me—less of Jesus. Please for Our Lady's sake do not tell or give anything . . . Let him write about "the work" and our poor suffering people—help me to pay for the schooling of our poor children and give the clever ones a chance in life.[5]

For Mother Teresa the work itself was the truth. She feared that if her subjective reflections entered the public world then people might lose sight of what really mattered. Mother Teresa never attempted to run away from her experience of divine loss, but neither did she let it destroy her. Rather she was able to find peace with it. She carried the wounds of her Crucifixion, neither hiding them nor showing them off.

Her strength is not staggering because she was able to banish all her doubts, but rather because she was able to acknowledge them without entering into some nihilistic prison. In her utter devotion to bringing life, protecting life, and enriching life, she utterly lost herself. And in losing herself she found joy, peace, happiness, and life.

In *Mere Christianity*, C. S. Lewis wrote, "This world is a great sculptor's shop. We are the statues, and there is a rumor going round the shop that some of us are some day going to come to life."[6] It is in meeting singular individuals like Mother Teresa that such a rumor is heard, for in her presence we not only witness life in all its fullness, but encounter the reality of our own deathly state.

In the Cross we witness both the destruction of religion and the sublimation of atheism. In the Garden of Gethsemane, Jesus forsakes everything for God (the highest religious gesture) but, on the Cross, we bear witness to Christ being forsaken by God (the atheistic moment). Then, in the Resurrection, we discover that God remains, *dwelling in our very midst through the embrace of life.* This is where the radical doubt of the Crucifixion is rendered sublime, where a new understanding of God is born and a type of a/theistic Christianity is glimpsed. We may call this new opening a/theism insomuch as we witness the move from traditional theism, through atheism to something that unifies and transcends them. A place where, as Bonhoeffer described, one takes full responsibility for one's existence as though God did not exist and, in fully doing so, lives fully before God.

If participation in the Crucifixion involves being overtaken by the darkness, where all guiding flames are extinguished, then participation in the Resurrection is the moment when we find the ability to affirm light and life in the very midst of the darkness and beneath the cold shadow of death. This is not some way of life that we can argue for as somehow better than the alternatives. We cannot find some reasoned apologetic for why one should embrace life in this way. Resurrection is not something one argues for, but it is the name we give to a mode of living.

Resurrection neither negates the Crucifixion nor moves beyond it. There is good reason why believers continue to wear a cross around their neck rather than dismiss it as something that lies forever behind them. The one who has participated in the Crucifixion remains indelibly marked by it. The Resurrection is a mode of life that arises from its very embrace.

Chapter Eight

Neither Christian nor Non-Christian

There once was a mother whose child tragically died only a few months after birth. The woman was so distraught by what had taken place that she carefully wrapped the infant's body in cloth and went in search of someone who would be able to resuscitate her.

She traveled far and wide to see doctors, magicians, and wisdom teachers, but none could offer any help. However, during her search, she heard rumors of a holy man who lived high up in the mountains, a man who possessed great powers. And so she went in search of this great saint, eventually locating his small dwelling in an isolated patch of land high above the city. Upon meeting him, she relayed her story through tears. After she had finished, the old man thought for a moment and then spoke with compassion, saying, "I can help you, but in order for me to do the appropriate spell, you will first need to bring me a handful of mustard seeds from the home of someone who has not suffered the pain of loss."

The woman immediately left that place and traveled throughout the city in search of a home that had not been overshadowed by this pain. However she could not find a single place. Yet as she heard the stories of others' suffering she slowly began to come to terms with her own, until one day she was able to give her beloved child a proper burial.[1]

Neither/Nor

The apostle Paul was by far the earliest Christian writer (his epistles predate the earliest gospel), yet he is almost completely silent about the teachings and miracles ascribed to Jesus. While Paul would have been well aware that he was the first person to write about the faith, he does not spend any time noting down what we might expect. He spends no time recording the sayings of his Lord and makes no effort to carefully preserve the various things people claimed he had done.

This is not what we might imagine the first Christian charged with writing about the faith would do, and so it requires an explanation. Very simply, Paul deeply understood that a community founded in the aftermath of Christ does not stand or fall on the teachings or miracles ascribed to Jesus. As a learned man, he knew very well that Jesus' teachings were mostly not new or innovative. He was offering an interpretation of the Hebrew Scriptures much like other rabbis' interpretations, and while some were powerful, Paul knew that salvation did not rest in adopting some teaching.

More than this Paul understood that the miracle claims were not unique to Jesus. Like many at that time, Paul would have been well aware that many of the miracles attributed to Jesus had also been attributed to others before, during, and after him (for instance, Caesar Augustus was said to have been born of a virgin).

The point is not to argue that these parts of Jesus' life had no interest for Paul, but to show that they were not central for him. For Paul, adherence to a set of teachings or belief in certain supernatural events in and of themselves meant nothing—*Conversion* was central to Christianity, and this meant participating in Crucifixion and Resurrection.

For Paul this meant something very precise. In the same way that Christ was stripped of his grounding identities, so Paul informs us that we must undergo the same process. He articulated this clearly in the following reflection:

> *You are all sons of God through faith in Christ Jesus, for all of you who were baptized into Christ have been clothed with Christ. There is neither Jew nor Greek, slave nor free, male nor female, for you are all one in Christ Jesus.*[2]

Each of these categories (Jew/Greek, slave/free, male/female) represented fundamental divisions that existed at the time. Jew/Greek described religious divisions, slave/free described political divisions and male/female described biological divisions. One's location in each of these categories described one's place, role, and value in society. These divisions were seen to be divinely given and part of the natural order. But Paul's radical message was that, in Christ, these identities are robbed of their defining power. Paul is here describing how Christianity cuts across all political, cultural, and biological divisions, rendering them null.

This did not mean that there were no longer men or women any more than it meant that there were no longer slaves or free. It meant, however, that these categories no longer defined the scope and limitations of one's world; the Christian community was called to experience the loss of their power and the liberation that resulted.

In other words, Paul was saying that these earthly distinctions were no longer to define or constrain us. In the new collective founded on Christ, these identities are to be radically cut through.

Paul makes this point very clearly by referring to the fundamental divisions of his day (Jew/Greek, slave/free, male/female). But it would be a mistake to think that Paul is referring only to these concrete expressions of religious, political, and biological divisions. We remain true to Paul's message only by including the various identities that define *our* place, role, and value in society today. This means saying that, in the community founded on Christ, there is neither black nor white, neither rich nor poor, neither powerful nor powerless. More than this we can add that there is neither Republican nor Democrat, liberal nor conservative, orthodox nor heretic. Indeed, in the spirit of the text, we must push further:

> You are all children of God through faith in Christ Jesus,
> for all of you who were baptized into Christ have clothed
> yourselves with Christ. There is neither high church nor low

church, Catholic nor Protestant, citizen nor alien, capitalist nor communist, gay nor straight, beautiful nor ugly, East nor West, theist nor atheist, Israel nor Palestine, American nor Iraqi, married nor divorced, uptown nor downtown, terrorist nor freedom fighter, for all are made one in Christ Jesus.

The Identity of No Identity

This vision of Paul's is often domesticated by those who would wish to turn this radical vision on its head and claim that he really means we must lay down all earthly identities in order to take up *another* identity, that of being a Christian. All identities are thus rendered impotent in relation to this unique super-identity. However, what if Paul is not saying that there is one identity that renders all others moot, but rather that in the very giving up of all our identities, we identify directly with Christ? Here Christianity is not yet another positive identity/worldview/mythology that can be placed alongside all others but is rather the name we give to the act of laying these down. The Christian community is not then distinct because it embraced yet another identity, but rather is unique in the way that its members lay down the various identities that would otherwise define them. This reading claims that Paul is directly attacking the unyielding social divisions that existed in his day, divisions that ensured some people (Jew, free, male) had more access to the true and the good than others (Gentile, slave, female).

In this way Paul saw the Cross as the event that opened up a way of living that was an alternative to the dominant principles of this world. It was then, as it is now, a scandal and a stumbling block because it ruptured the various divisions of the day, exposing them as contingent rather than divinely ordained.

In theological terms, this giving up of identity can be described as participating in *kenosis,* a theological term that describes the divine renunciation of all power and privilege. It refers to the self-emptying of God that we see expressed so beautifully both through the Incarnation and the Crucifixion. Something we see described expressly in Philippians when we read,

> *Your attitude should be the same as that of Christ Jesus: Who, being in very nature God, did not consider equality with God something to be grasped, but made himself nothing.* [3]

In this way we can read Paul's statement in the book of Galatians as a description of how, in the very act of becoming nothing, we identify with Christ. We can even say that in Christ there is neither Christian nor non-Christian—for the word "Christian" itself now refers to the embrace of a concrete identity, with a concrete mythology, rather than to the renunciation of these.

IN THIS SPACE OF NEITHER/NOR that Paul reveals, we experience others (and ourselves) in a fundamentally different way. The Jewish philosopher Emmanuel Levinas summarized what this might look like in an interview when he commented that, if we see the color of someone's eyes, we are not relating to them. That is, if we are not listening to someone, we will be well aware of external features such as the color of their eyes, the clothes they are wearing, etc. However, once we get into a deep and intimate conversation, we no longer notice these external features. It is not that they have become invisible, but we enter into an "I/ Thou" relationship in which we encounter the other in such a way that they are no longer reducible to various properties. We encounter the other beyond the color of their eyes, the quality of their clothes, and the specific nature of their political and religious commitments.

Identifying with Christ, then, does not involve a way of adding some new interpretation to the world, but rather involves an act of subtraction in which we lay aside our various interpretations of the world.

It is vital to note here that Paul is not primarily concerned with people intellectually acknowledging that our various identities fail to define us. Such an idea is already popular in today's world. We in the West already view our relation to our various identities in a rather cynical way. For instance, I don't really believe in a consumerist vision of the world and even ridicule the messages that the advertisements and magazines bombard me with, but, as I've previously explored, this intellectual rejection does not prevent my direct and total participation in these identities. We don't have to believe in the various roles that are given to us by our political, religious, and social context; we can even laugh at them. The problem is that even amidst our conscious rejection, they still exhibit their power and thus continue to define how we use our time, resources, and energy. I might not feel myself constrained by some social, political, or religious identity, but I still am constrained in my actual practices. Isn't this what we see in *The Sims, Second Life*, and other role-playing games? Here we are free to try on a variety of different personas, feeling that none really define us, and yet, when we come out of the game, we still fit neatly into the pattern cut out for us by the dominant religious, political, and social environment.

The vision expressed by Paul is markedly different from this. Drawing directly as it does from the Crucifixion and Resurrection of Christ, it is not concerned with some intellectual recognition that we must affirm, but rather with a deeply felt experience that we undergo—one in which our various culturally given identities are stripped of their operative power. The scandalous nature of this radical vision is captured succinctly in the Gospel according to John, where the Christian is described as one who lives in the world (with all of its social, religious, and political divisions) while no longer being of it (not being held fast by them).[4]

This is why the argument that we cannot live without such identities misses the point. Of course, an opaque biological, socio-symbolic background constitutes us; of course, we cannot forget our gender, sexual preferences, political opinions, nationality, etc. But while being within them, we can find ourselves no longer *of* them. In other words, we can occupy a space in which they are no longer the absolute horizon. We *see* them rather than simply see through them.

A collective founded upon Crucifixion and Resurrection invites people into the experience of this neither/nor, not by offering signs that point toward this reality (like a road sign), but by offering sacramental and liturgical performances that open up a participation in it.

Paul's vision is not then an ideal that points to some future epoch, a heavenly existence lying beyond the present in which there will be no division. For such a view actually helps to maintain present inequalities. Take the example of those who did not oppose the ideal of equality of women but felt that one couldn't let women vote here and now because they were not properly educated. The argument was that there should be equality and that one day there would be, but first so many other things had to be changed. Sexism was thus masked in a seeming concern for the plight of women and a concern for society.

What Paul instead describes is a way of life that starts *right here and right now*, in the very midst of the world. We enact Crucifixion and Resurrection here in the place where we currently stand.

Don't Fulfill Your Dreams

When this loss of identity is enacted in a liturgical setting, we may call it a suspended space, for in that location one symbolically leaves one's identities at the door. In this space we are no longer constrained by the ambition of creating a world where we can fulfill our dreams. The problem with this ambition is simply that the dreams themselves arise within a particular context and reflect our current identities. They are formed from a social, political, and religious matrix that is, for the most part, utterly transparent to us. This matrix then provides the scope and limitations of what we can imagine and hope for. As such our dreams reflect back in a concrete way the particular abstract values embedded in this opaque background.

A clear example of how this works can be seen in the fairy tales that we tell our children. These fairy tales are more than mere stories to help a child fall asleep; they reflect the values of our society (whether good or bad) and provide a powerful means of passing these values on to the next generation. Traditional Western fairy tales, as mythological expressions of our values, are often concerned with poor people becoming wealthy, powerless people becoming powerful, or single people finding a suitable marriage partner. This is very different from cultures that have stories of the rich renouncing their wealth, the powerful becoming weak, and lovers letting their beloved go. The stories we tell our children will thus tell us something about our own values and the values of the system that we are embedded in. They are then both a manifestation of underlying societal norms and a powerful means of passing those norms on.

Just as this is true of a society's fairy tales, so it is true of our personal ideals, political dreams, and religious imaginings. Our ideas of what a fulfilled life would look like, how a just society would operate, or how an authentic faith could be expressed are all too often uncritically reflective of the dominant underlying political and theological ideas that we imbibed as infants. The truly revolutionary move, then, does not lie in attempting to fulfill our dreams but in putting ourselves into a situation in which we are able to dream new ones.

This is pyro-theology, insomuch as it sees the unchanging truth of faith nestled not in any positive claims to reality but in the ongoing testing and transformation of those claims through the fires of passionate, loving debate. The truth of faith is not then to be found in some new movement but in the antagonism that generates the birth of new movements. The truth is not found in the conservative, liberal, evangelical, fundamentalist, or orthodox traditions but in the spaces between these traditions and in the gaps that exist within them—gaps which open them up to ever new and apocalyptic possibilities.

This is why revolutionaries are always untimely—for the simple reason that they can never be deemed reasonable or right by the present system because it is the present system that they critique. Consider a group of activists who protest against the building of a highway through a forest. It is perfectly possible to find many, if not most, of the protesters acknowledging both the futility of their mission and even questioning its justification. The protesters may know that, on purely rational grounds, the highway is needed. They may know that, were they to engage in a public debate, their position would be exposed as lacking the rational framework that would justify their actions. Why? Because the presently accepted way of understanding the world dictates the scope and limitations of the rational framework itself.

So why do they act? Because they are affirming a reality that does not yet exist, a reality that would, if it was initiated, justify the actions that they are presently engaged in. They are fighting without justification for a world that would one day offer that justification. A world that, if ever realized, would itself need to be critiqued and transformed by others.

Truth Is Conflict

The liturgical enactment of suspended space draws us into an environment where we can begin to free ourselves of the dreams that we have been raised on and begin to dream new ones, something that will involve imaging, debating, and enacting genuinely alternative modes of community. The liturgical space invites us to step out of the world we currently inhabit in the hope that we will be able to step back into it with a vision for its further transformation. This stands in contrast to either renouncing the present values of the world or trying to fulfill them. Instead, we conceptualize alternative worlds and conjure up new landscapes, all of which can and should themselves be challenged. For the truth is not located in one position or the other, neither is the truth some calm overarching whole that contains all the various conflicting ideas. *The truth arises in the very conflict itself, the conflict that drives us onward.*

The insurrectionary event of Christian faith brings us into the very heart of truth by freeing us from the dominant ideologies of our culture. Is this not what we see clearly and concisely expressed by Paul himself when he writes,

> *From now on those who have wives should live as if they had none; those who mourn, as if they did not; those who are happy, as if they were not; those who buy something, as if it were not theirs to keep; those who use the things of the world, as if not engrossed in them. For this world in its present form is passing away.*[5]

Here we see that our relationships, emotions, and possessions, while part of our life, are no longer allowed to dictate our existence. We are asked to embrace the world while never being fully identified with it. In a famous analysis, the philosopher Jean-Paul Sartre wrote of a waiter in a Parisian cafe whose actions were so exaggerated that he became a caricature of what we imagine a Parisian waiter to be. Sartre noted how the waiter was not merely doing his job, but rather fully identifying with it. For Sartre this was a type of bad faith—for the individual is never reducible to his or her social role.[6] We may do the job of waiter, but we should never consider ourselves waiters. In the same way, we may attend a Presbyterian church, but we should never think of ourselves as Presbyterians.

The Centrality of Absence

In order to invite people into this liturgical space, one needs to reflect the experience of loss in the structure itself. Authentic collectives based upon the Crucifixion and Resurrection, then, will be marked out by the way that they reflect this central experience in their prayers, music, and liturgies—not only questioning social, political, and church identities (as we see in Christ, who was abandoned by his friends, the religious community, and the political system) but in bringing about the very loss of any ultimate grounding (as we see in Christ's cry to God). As an example of the type of music that might draw people into this sacred place, take Pádraig Ô Tuama's worship song "Maranatha" from the album *Hymns to Swear By,* a song that is composed of words and phrases taken directly from the laments of Jeremiah,

> *You are strength but I am weak*
> *You are strength but I am weak*
> *You are strength but I am weak*
> *Maranatha*
> *Maranatha*
> *Maranatha*

> *I've given up sometimes when I've been tired*
> *I've given up sometimes when I've been tired*
> *I've given up sometimes when I've been tired*
> *Does it move you*
> *Does it move you*
> *Does it move you*

> *I curse the day when I received the light*

I curse the day when I received the light
I curse the day when I received the light
When you deceived me
When you deceived me
When you deceived me

I've f—— it up so many times
I've f—— it up so many times
I've f—— it up so many times
Hallelujah
Hallelujah
Hallelujah

I've found my home in Babylon
I've found my home in Babylon
I've found my home in Babylon
Here in exile
Here in exile
Here in exile[7]

This is not simply a song *about* suffering and the sense of cosmic homelessness—it is sung *from* that space, remains *within* that space, and renders that space palpable. It is a song that invites us to connect with the depth of our suffering rather than running from it or trying to cover over it. This is an act that can be deeply cathartic, for just as a melancholic love song can help us access our own lost loves and unlock our own pain in a healthy way, so such worship can help us to face up to the feelings of loss, meaningless-ness, and guilt in a way that is not overwhelming. It can provide a ritualistic expression that enables us to face our suffering and un-knowing without being overcome by it and falling into despair.

It can be so hard to give up on easy answers and face up to our feelings of finitude, meaninglessness, and guilt. But it is not the role of the Christian community to provide some escape from these; rather such a community offers a way for us to confront them and affirm them together.

It is this that we bear witness to in the parable that describes the woman with her deceased infant. She is suffering so much that she seeks a way to avoid the reality through any means necessary. The holy man understands that the child has gone and nothing will bring her back, yet he avoids two unhelpful traps: the first, to simply say that nothing can be done and send the woman on her way; the second, to use this as an opportunity to introduce the crutch of religion. Instead, he realizes that this woman needs to face up to the pain and work through it.

In this parable the holy man is able to bring the woman into contact with others who have also suffered, people who are able to bear witness to the pain that befell this mother and connect in some way with it. This woman was not in a place where she could have taken the direct advice to talk with others—she wanted the pain to be gone in an instant. But regardless of what she wanted, what she needed was to meet with others who could share her suf-fering and talk with those who could connect with her story in all of its darkness and distress.

Instead of offering some system of explanation for what had happened, the appropriate response lay in creating a space for deep, honest, and compassionate human interaction. In the same way, it is not the job the community of faith to offer ways of escaping the suffering that is part of being human (namely the anxiety brought about by the sense of death, meaninglessness, and guilt), but rather to form spaces in which it can be acknowledged and worked through.

It is a community fully embracing life in all its joy and pain that is faithful to the way of Christ. Something that is expressed in the work of Bonhoeffer when, in prison and facing imminent death, he wrote about a worldly Christianity, saying,

> By this-worldliness I mean living unreservedly in life's duties, problems, successes and failures, experiences and perplexities. In so doing we throw ourselves completely into the arms of God, taking seriously, not our own suffering, but those of God in the world—watching with Christ in Gethsemane. That, I think, is faith, that is metanoia [conversion]; and that is how one becomes a man and a Christian.[8]

Becoming the Resurrection

In light of all this, to deny the Resurrection of Christ means nothing less than to turn away from the world, to run from our suffering, to avoid an authentic meeting with our neighbor, and to hide from ourselves. It means holding too tightly to what we have and identifying too closely with our idealized image. It means avoiding doubt, turning from our weakness, and refusing to face up to our finitude. In short, it means saying "no" to life.

For most of us this means that we deny the Resurrection on a daily basis, regardless of what we confess with our lips.

But then there are times when we may affirm it: times when we embrace life, face up to our pain, allow ourselves to mourn. Times when we meet our neighbor, look at ourselves without fear, take responsibility for our actions, listen to our fears, find joy in the simplest of things, and gain pleasure through embracing the broken world. In times like these, we say "yes" to life and, in doing so, we say "yes" to Christ. For it is only when we are the site where Resurrection takes place that we truly affirm it. To believe in the Crucifixion and Resurrection means nothing less than enacting them.

Go in Pieces

The task is ended
Go in pieces
Our faith has been rear-ended
Certainty amended
And something might be mended
That we didn't know was torn

And we are fire—bright, burning fire
Turning from the higher places
From which we fell
Emptying ourselves into the hell
In which we'll find
Our loving and beloved
Brother, mother, sister, father, friend

And so, friends, the task is ended
Go in pieces to see and feel your world

Rob Bell Interviews Peter Rollins

In 2009, Rob Bell invited Peter Rollins to participate in a three-day conference entitled Poets, Prophets and Preachers. During this time Rob interviewed Peter about some of the themes that would later find expression in this book. As such we have included the full interview for you to watch and share.

Use your Smartphone to scan this code to unlock the full-length video of Rob Bell interviewing Pete Rollins

Acknowledgments

We are a gift that is given to us by the ones we love. For the very person we are today has come to be through the influences of those who have nurtured, taught, inspired, challenged, and supported us. Their visions and desires find a home within us and fuse with our flesh in such a way as to bring whole new worlds into being.

I am so very lucky to have the unique constellation of family and friends that I do. I am indebted and know that any treasure I have to offer has been pillaged from them.

In relation to the book that you hold in your hands, I would like to specifically mention some of the people who helped it come into being. My heartfelt thanks go to Brian and Jill Olson for their overwhelming support, advice, and kindness, Greg Daniel for believing in the message, Becky Nesbitt for preparing the way for its publication, and Andy Meisenheimer for making sure that it was polished and ready. I also want to thank Jay Bakker and the Rev. Vince Anderson for their friendship as I settled into a new and foreign land. But most importantly I must thank "Eleven," who is the real inspiration and source of all my work.

Notes

Introduction: There Is a Fire Inside the Building; Please Step Inside

1. Dietrich Bonhoeffer, *Witness to Jesus Christ,* ed. John De Gruchy (San Francisco: Collins, 1987), 278.
2. Dietrich Bonhoeffer, *Letters and Papers from Prison* (New York: Touchstone, 1971), 280–82.
3. Ibid., 282.
4. Slavoj Žižek, "Soul of the Party," *New Statesman,* April 1, 2010.

Chapter 1: I'm a Christian! I'm a Christian!

1. Colossians 2:8.

Chapter 2: To Believe Is Human; to Doubt, Divine

1. Adapted from an Islamic parable.
2. Matthew 27:46 and Mark 15:34.
3. Matthew 26:36–46.
4. Elie Wiesel, *Night* (New York: Bantam Books, 1982), 62.
5. Elizabeth Anscombe, *An Introduction to Wittgenstein's Tractatus* (London: Harper & Row, 1959), 151.
6. p. 36 The Prisoner.
7. Friedrich Nietzsche, *Thus Spoke Zarathustra,* trans. R. J. Hollingdale (London: Penguin, 1969), 103.
8. Luke 14:26.
9. Slavoj Žižek, *Living in the End Times* (London: Verso, 2010), 115.

Chapter 3: "I'm Not Religious" and Other Religious Sayings

1. Richard Woods, *Meister Eckhart* (London: Continuum, 2011), 130.
2. As I remember from hearing him share the story in person.

Chapter 4: I Don't Have to Believe; My Pastor Does That for Me

1. Søren Kierkegaard, *Either/Or,* trans. Alastair Hannay (London: Penguin, 1992), 43.

2. Albert C. Outler and Richard P. Heitzenrater, eds., *John Wesley's Sermons* (Nashville: Abingdon Press, 1987), 69–84.
3. Brian Kolodiejchuk, M.C., ed., *Mother Teresa: Come Be My Light* (New York: Doubleday, 2007), 210.
4. 1 Corinthians 15:19.

CHAPTER 5: STORY CRIME
1. Slavoj Žižek, *How to Read Lacan* (London: Granta Books, 2006), 58.
2. *Homes and Gardens,* November 1938, 193–95.
3. Matthew 6:24.
4. Bonhoeffer, *Witness to Jesus Christ,* 288.
5. Ibid., 289.
6. Mark 14:27–31.
7. Mark 14:66–72.
8. 1 Corinthians 6:12.

CHAPTER 6: WE ARE DESTINY
1. Ancient Hindu parable.
2. 1 Corinthians 15:55.
3. *Journals and Papers of Søren Kierkegaard.*
4. Bonhoeffer, *Witness to Jesus Christ,* 112–13.
5. *The Gay Science,* section 341.
6. Matthew 18:19–20.

CHAPTER 7: I BELIEVE IN THE INSURRECTION
1. Ephesians 6:12.
2. For more about Pirate Islands and faith see Kester Brewin, *Other: Loving Self, God and Neighbor in a World of Fractures* (London: Hodder & Stoughton, 2010).
3. Thomas Merton, *The Hidden Ground of Love,* William H. Shannon, ed. (Toronto: Collins, 1985), 111.
4. Brian Kolodiejchuk, ed., *Mother Teresa: Come Be My Light* (New York: Doubleday, 2007), 349.
5. Ibid., 5–6.
6. C. S. Lewis, *Mere Christianity* (New York: HarperCollins, 2007), 131.

CHAPTER 8: NEITHER CHRISTIAN NOR NON-CHRISTIAN
1. Adapted from an ancient Buddhist parable.
2. Galatians 3:26–28.
3. Philippians 2:5–7a.
4. John 15:19.
5. 1 Corinthians 7:29b–31.
6. Jean-Paul Sartre, *Being and Nothingness* (London: Methuen & Co., Ltd., 1969), 59.
7. Pádraig Ó Tuama, *Hymns to Swear By* (Proost: 2010).
8. Bonhoeffer, *Witness to Jesus Christ,* 294.

Reading Group Guide

Introduction

In striking contrast to many of today's feel-good evangelists, author Peter Rollins asserts that the traditional church has become little more than a security blanket for the faithful—comforting but ultimately meaningless. To move beyond this infantile kind of faith, Rollins invites Christians to participate fully with Christ on the cross and his deeply authentic cry, "My God, my God, why have you forsaken me?" Only in doing so, Rollins says, can Christians bring about the radical changes sorely needed for the church to bring God's love to a hurting world.

Topics & Questions for Discussion

1. Reflect a moment on your personal beliefs about God, Jesus Christ, and religion in general. How did you come to hold these beliefs? Where did they originate?

2. Peter Rollins discusses what he calls "Circumcision Questions." (p. xii) What is the meaning of this term and how does it impact the life of the church? What do you think is the Circumcision Question set forth in *Insurrection,* and what potential effect do you think it could have on the church as you know it?

3. Rollins builds on the late Dietrich Bonhoeffer's idea of "whether or not *religion* is necessary in order to participate fully in the life testified to by Christ." (p. xiv) How would you answer this question and why, based on your own experience?

4. What is meant by "pyro-theology"? (p. xv) What purpose does pyro-theology serve? In your opinion, do the ideas expressed in *Insurrection* qualify as pyro-theology? Why or why not?

5. Concerning God, Rollins writes that "(w)e find great solace in the idea of someone presiding over the world who guarantees that our small and insignificant lives are being seen and cherished." (p. 7) To that end, he quotes Voltaire: "If God did not exist, it would be necessary to invent him." What do you think of these ideas? Do you agree or not? Explain your response.

6. Thinking back over your current and/or past church experiences, do you agree with the author that the church performs the same function as a child's security blanket? (p. 48) Why or why not?

7. What is meant by Rollins's statement, "humans are able to affirm one thing consciously while affirming the opposite thing in the way they live"? (p. 44) To what extent do you think that this is true of the church today? If you can, describe a time when you've seen this principle in action.

8. Explain how it might be possible that someone could hold no personal religious beliefs, and yet find comfort and solace in the beliefs of someone else. (p. 57)

9. Describe what you think it means to participate in Christ's Crucifixion. Is your view of this participation in sync with the author's? (p. 23) Explain.

10. What is meant by a God who operates "deus ex machina"? (p. 12) Do you believe that God acts in this way? Provide an example to support your answer.

11. What does it mean to "ridicule the religious view of God while affirming this God in our practice"? (p. 50) To what extent, if any, does this describe your own faith experience?

12. The author says that "When we are directly confronted by what we know, but have refused to admit, we can no longer pretend that we are ignorant." (p. 68) Did this book confront you with anything you already knew, but chose not to see? If so, explain.

13. The author states, "Paul deeply understood that a community founded in the aftermath of Christ does not stand or fall on the teachings or miracles ascribed to Jesus." (p. 164) Do you agree? What else would such a community be founded on?

14. Rollins equates affirming the Resurrection with "times when we embrace life, face up to our pain, allow ourselves to mourn, . . . meet our neighbor, look at ourselves without fear, take responsibility for our actions, find joy in the simplest of things, and gain pleasure through embracing the broken world." (p. 180) To what extent does this view reflect your own understanding of the Resurrection?

ENHANCE YOUR BOOK GROUP

1. Brainstorm as a group what a truly post-religious church would look and sound like. Who would attend and why? What kinds of songs would be sung? What would the preaching be like? List as many details as you can.

2. When you've finished brainstorming, share whatever thoughts and feelings came up during the process. Did you find the exercise easy or difficult? Did envisioning a new kind of church make you feel optimistic? Pessimistic? Anxious? Hopeful? All of the above? Why?

3. Discuss whether, on the whole, you think that this type of faith community is a worthy goal to work toward. Why or why not?

4. If you favor the idea of a radically different kind of church, think of some ways that you, as an individual and as a group, could help bring it about. Is there a specific action that you can take this month? This week? Today?

5. Visit peterrollins.net to learn more about the author and his work.

A CONVERSATION WITH PETER ROLLINS

How does the title, *Insurrection,* relate to the central question or concept presented in your book?

I am interested in playing with and drawing out the similarity that exists between the words "Insurrection" and "Resurrection." At a very basic level, one describes an uprising and the other a rising up. My desire is to show the reader that there is a close link between the theological idea of Resurrection and the idea of an Insurrection: in other words, the core proclamation of Christianity is that we can live in a radically different way. This is the way of love, and it is a way that embraces others and says "yes" to life and births within us a courage to take responsibility for our existence. This book is about saying that Christianity invites us to embrace a life before death, a life that is rich, beautiful, and so free that its very existence is a challenge to any system of oppression.

What factors inspired or compelled you to write *Insurrection* at this time? Do you feel it contains a message of particular significance "for such a time as this" in the history of the church?

The short answer is "yes." I believe that the church is a living community that ought to be involved in perpetual revolution and that this will manifest itself in different ways at different times in its historical life. I believe that this is a moment in history when we need to challenge the way in which church in all its forms (Orthodox, Evangelical, Catholic, Liberal and Conservative and Fundamentalist) employs the idea of God and understand the meaning of faith. This is a huge task and one that will prove very difficult, but I believe it is essential if the church is not only to survive, but become an instrument of positive change in the world.

Have you experienced any kind of resistance when you've shared the idea of pyro-theology with others?

Perhaps first and foremost I have experienced resistance from myself. The idea that I need to radically interrogate the things that I hold dear and encounter my own brokenness, darkness, and vulnerability is terrifying. My religious narrative gives me a sense that I am right, that I am master, that I know the secret meaning of the universe. I don't want to give that up, I don't want to encounter the truth that I am human, all too human. I know that others feel resistance to the idea, but I speak first and foremost to myself. If I am not prepared to place myself into the fires of pyro-theology, then I cannot expect anyone else to. Most of the resistance that I experience is not from people who simply write me off but actually people who say that they are frightened. I know what they mean. It is frightening. All I can say is that I walk the same path, that I have found liberation there, and that I believe it is this path that remains most faithful to the heart of Christianity.

Did the process of writing this book uncover any surprises for you, or take you down a path you didn't expect?

In my experience the first person a book educates is the author herself. Writing feels to me like cutting a path through a landscape. It seems like you could go in any direction at first but there are blockages all around. These not only curb the direction you take but mean that you might not end up where you initially wanted. The blockages in the landscape are the places that reason, logic, and reflection cannot take you. As you cut through the undergrowth, it becomes clear that you have to make twists and turns you could never have anticipated before embarking on the journey. Sure, I have an idea of where it might go, and I will have spent months reading and reflecting before I begin to put pen to paper, but for me, one of the most exciting things about writing is the way it brings me to places I could never before have imagined.

What changes do you hope to see in the church as a result of this book? What impact might these ideas have on the practice of worship, ministry, and community?

I would love to see churches take seriously the idea that mystery, unknowing, brokenness, doubt, and mourning should be expressed in the very structure of the church itself. Religion is a system that gives us a sense of being right, of having the answers and knowing how to stay on the right team. I want to see churches that break religion open through the sermons, music, and prayers; churches that bring us face-to-face with the truth of our unknowing and pain. Not so that we despair, but so that, in bringing it to light and sharing it, we can find healing and light. I would love to see churches emphasize that the highest principle is not some object that we need to love, but rather the act of love itself. That in loving we break open the depth and beauty of what we mean when we say "God."

This will be difficult for churches to do because people often go there to escape their suffering and darkness rather than have it exposed. But the church should be like the singer-songwriter we might listen to when we are working through a difficult situation. They sing their sorrowful song, and, in doing so, we confront our own suffering in a way that is painful without being overpowering. As we sit there and listen to the music, we are invited to work through our pain, engage in the act of mourning, and find strength in the midst of our weakness. Then when we leave, we are in a better state than when we arrived. Sadly, the church is too often like the most inane kind of pop music. Here the music makes us feel strong and powerful, effectively obscuring the sadness within us. Yet when we leave the concert we realize that we have not worked through our pain but merely avoided a direct confrontation with it for a while.

Do you think that the post-religious church will resemble the first-century church more closely than most modern churches do? If so, in what ways?

No. In fact I think that the desire to resemble the first-century church is fundamentally misguided. This desire comes from the idea that they were somehow closer to the event housed in Christianity than we are; that this event lies in the distant past and that we need to resemble that past in order to recover that event. The fact is that the event that birthed the Christian faith does not lie in the past but is right here, right now.

This event is so powerful that, when incarnated, this reality will give birth to radically new communities that may not look anything like what went before them, even though they are fed by the same blood. The task is not to return to the early church, but rather to return to the event that gave birth to the early church.

What do you see as the role of the Bible in the post-religious church?

The Bible is the central text for Christians just as other texts are central to other groups (the writings of Marx for Marxists etc.). The Bible describes a way of living and being that those who love that book believe gets at a fundamental truth. Like all communities with central texts, Christians will continue to do what they have always done: read it, wrestle with it, argue with it, systematize it, interpret it, deconstruct it, and find meaning within it. Sadly this kinetic, dynamic, and living relationship with the text is something that religion condemns, because its closed system of belief is threatened by such a fluid relationship with the text.

What is the primary message you hope readers will take away from *Insurrection*?

I guess that life before death is possible; that you don't need to hide from yourself, pretending that you are not unhappy, broken, and fearful of various things. That you can face up to these things and learn to live with them and that you can say yes to life. I want people to know that beyond the naïveté of believing we can be fulfilled and that beyond the despair of knowing we cannot is a Resurrection road. A narrow path along which we learn to travel together, making space for our darkness and humanity, finding healing in the very embrace of our wounds and sustenance in the very acceptance of our hunger.

What would you say to the reader who is deeply moved by *Insurrection* and wonders "what's the next step" toward changing the way church happens?

I would encourage the reader to be part of a revolution that is attempting to change the structure of the church itself. If they write music, I would encourage them to pen deeply human songs for worship. If they preach, I would ask them to be honest about their doubts in front of those they stand before. If they write prayers, then I would invite them to include anger, unknowing, and lament in the constructions. I would encourage those who attend church to let their leaders know that they want them to express their humanity in public, that they want to be part of a church that has humility and self-critique at its heart. And perhaps most of all, I would encourage the reader to seek out others on this journey, because the path can be a lonely one.

Do you have another book project in the works?

Yes. I have a few actually. Currently I feel that I am in a very fertile period in my writing. I have been experimenting with writing philosophical fairy tales, a book exploring what I believe to be the core message that runs through the Hebrew and Christian scriptures, and also a book that looks at how we put some of the ideas found in Insurrection into practice. As time goes on, some of these projects may merge together. Watch this space . . .